BITCOIN, CYRPTOCURRENCY, AND BLOCKCHAIN

HOW TO GET STARTED

Springbrook Publishing
Dayton, Ohio

DISCLAIMER

This book has been written for information purposes only. Every effort has been made to make it as complete and accurate as possible. It provides information only up to the publishing date. Therefore, this book should be used as a guide and not as an ultimate source.

The publisher does warrant that the information contained in this book is fully complete and shall not be responsible for any errors or omissions. The publisher shall have neither liability nor responsibility to any person or entity with respect to any loss or damage caused or alleged to be caused directly or indirectly by this book.

TABLE OF CONTENTS

INTRODUCTION

Bitcoin (₿) is a cryptocurrency invented in 2008 by an unknown person or group of people using the name Satoshi Nakamoto. The currency began use in 2009 when its implementation was released as open-source software.

Bitcoin is a decentralized digital currency, without a central bank or single administrator, that can be sent from user to user on the peer-to-peer bitcoin network without the need for intermediaries. Transactions are verified by network nodes through cryptography and recorded in a public distributed ledger called a blockchain. Bitcoins are created as a reward for a process known as mining. They can be exchanged for other currencies, products, and services. Research produced by the University of Cambridge estimated that in 2017, there were 2.9 to 5.8 million unique users using a cryptocurrency wallet, most of them using bitcoin. Bitcoin has been criticized for its use in illegal transactions, the large amount of electricity used by miners, price volatility, and thefts from exchanges. Some economists, including several Nobel laureates, have characterized it as a speculative bubble at various times. Bitcoin has also been used as an investment, although several regulatory agencies have issued investor alerts about bitcoin.

Source: *https://en.wikipedia.org/wiki/Bitcoin*

SECTION 1: BITCOIN

Description of Bitcoin

Bitcoin is a digital and global money system currency. It allows people to send or receive money across the internet, even to someone they don't know or don't trust. Money can be exchanged without being linked to a real identity. The mathematical field of cryptography is the basis for Bitcoin's security.

Bitcoin was invented by someone using the name **Satoshi Nakamoto**. A Bitcoin address, or simply address, is an identifier of 26-35 letters and numbers, beginning with the number 1 or 3, that represents a possible destination for a bitcoin payment. Addresses can be generated at no cost by any user of Bitcoin. For example, using Bitcoin Core, one can click "New Address" and be assigned an address. It is also possible to get a Bitcoin address using an account at an exchange or online wallet service.

There are currently two address formats in common use:

Common P2PKH which begin with the number 1; e.g.: 1BvBMSEstWetqTFn5Au4m4GFg7xJaNVN2.

Newer P2SH type starting with the number 3; e.g.: 3MXknxVapwv6QkMoQv99MBuXZ2XpPewHn9.

Source: *https://simple.wikipedia.org/wiki/Bitcoin*

How to Acquire Bitcoin

There are many different techniques to acquiring Bitcoins, and in this guide, we will show you the most popular methods of getting yourself some units of the world's most popular cryptocurrency.

Purchasing Bitcoin

Purchasing Bitcoins is a very straightforward process. Bitcoin can be purchased through an exchange such as Coinbase Pro, Robinhood, Gemini, and Kraken. Fiat currency is exchanged to purchase Bitcoin. At the time of publishing you can expect to pay more than $50,000 for a single

NOTE: You do not have to purchase a whole Bitcoin. Each Bitcoin can be divided into 100 million units called Santoshi's. You can purchase a few thousand Santoshi's for a few dollars. This will not make you rich, but you can get a feel for how Bitcoins and cryptocurrency works.

Here are some of places where you can buy Bitcoins:

Cryptocurrency Exchanges

There are plenty of platforms where you can buy and sell cryptocurrency. The most popular ones that have been around a few years are Coinbase, Kraken, Robinhood and Gemini. Refer to Top 10 Spot Market Exchanges.

Cash Exchanges

Another payment method that's popular is the use cash exchanges like Local Bitcoin or Wall of Coins. These platforms allow you to trade directly with another person. There are lower transaction fees involved. However, they may charge a fee for successful trades. We would suggest that you look for a platform that offers an escrow service to make sure the seller doesn't run away with your hard-earned cash!

Trading Alternate Cryptocurrencies for Bitcoin

If you have a digital wallet with other cryptocurrencies, you can easily trade these for Bitcoins on a currency exchange. Coinbase, Kraken, Robinhood and Gemini are available if you create an account.

Receiving Payments with Bitcoins

To receive payments, you will need to create a Bitcoin wallet to start receiving payments. You can create a free online wallet on Coinbase, Kraken, Robinhood and Gemini.

A valid email address is needed to sign up and begin receiving payments. Once a wallet is set up, you can generate a QR code or use the long alphanumeric address and send it to the person you wish to receive Bitcoins from.

Storing Bitcoins.

Bitcoins are stored in digital wallets. The wallets exist in the cloud or on computers. A wallet is similar to a virtual bank account. The wallets allow individuals to send and/or receive Bitcoins, pay for items or save the bitcoins. The bitcoin wallets are never insured by the FDIC.

Types of Wallets.

Cloud Wallet

The advantage of having a wallet in the cloud is that people don't need to install any software in their computers and wait for long syncing processes. The disadvantage is that the cloud may be hacked and people may lose their bitcoins. Nevertheless, these sites are very secure.

Computer Wallet

The advantage of a wallet on a computer is that Bitcoins are secured from the rest of the internet. The disadvantage is they may by deleted by formatting the computer or because of viruses.

Example of a QR Code and Wallet Address

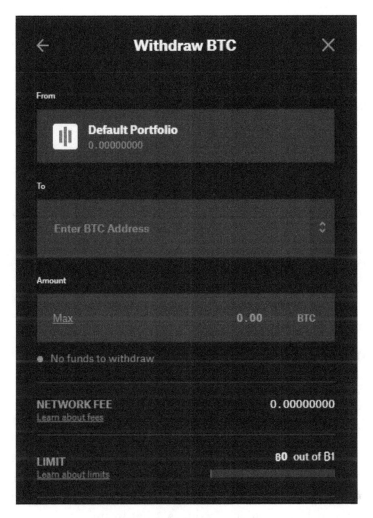

Example of a Withdraw Request

Payment Options for Bitcoin

Receiving Bitcoins for Work Performed

There are several types of work that might pay in Bitcoin. Sending and receiving Bitcoin payments is a straightforward process. When sending or receiving cryptocurrency always double check to ensure that the type of cryptocurrency being sent or received matches the type of wallet. This will result in permanent loss of the transaction on the network. For example: Do not send or receive Bitcoin (BTC) to a Ethereum (ETH) wallet or vice versa.

Receiving Tips

To receive tips from customers, you would give them your wallet address and they would deposit directly into your wallet address.

Transferring Bitcoin

Bitcoins can be sent with a smart phone, computers, or an online exchange.

Mining and Cloud Mining

The Bitcoin network is secured by the miners. They are rewarded for verified transactions. The network transactions are fully verified and then they are recorded in an a public ledger. The miners compete this by using computer software and hardware to solve difficult math problems. Cloud miners invest in third party mining companies which provide infrastructure which reduces hardware and energy consumption expenses.

Bitcoin Anonymity.

When executing a bitcoin transaction, there's no need to provide the real name of the person. Each one of the bitcoin transactions are recorded in a public log. This public log contains only wallet IDs and not names. so each transaction is private. You can buy and sell things without being tracked.

Bitcoin Innovation.

Bitcoin has established a new way of innovation. The bitcoin software is all open source, anyone can review it. A fact is Bitcoin is transforming the world's finances similar to how the web changed everything about publishing. Transaction fee reductions are a perk of Bitcoin.

Governmental Concerns About Bitcoin

Government agencies are increasingly worried about the implications of Bitcoin, as it has the ability to be used anonymously, and is therefore a potential instrument for money laundering. Law enforcers seem to be concerned about the decentralized nature of the currency.

Who Regulates Bitcoin?

Regulators will vary on a per-country basis and you can expect to see national financial regulators interested in Bitcoin and other cryptocurrencies.

Private Sector Companies (Banks)

Several banks have stopped accounts owned by people operating Bitcoin exchanges. In one case, a bank was unhappy that a company that was involved did not have a money transmitting business (MTB) account.

FinCEN

In the US, the Financial Crimes Enforcement Network (FinCEN) is an agency within the US Treasury Department that published guidelines about the use of virtual currencies.

FinCEN's March 18, 2013 guidance defines the circumstances under which crpytocurrency users could be categorized as money services businesses (also commonly known as money transmitting businesses or MTBs). MTBs must enforce Anti-Money Laundering (AML) and Know Your Client (KYC) measures, identifying the people that they're doing business with.

CFTC

The US Commodity Futures Trading Commission (CTFC) looks after financial derivatives.

SEC

The US Securities and Exchange Commission (SEC) has not issued regulations on virtual currencies.

United States Legislative Branch

The SEC case has forced the legislative branch of government to consider cryptocurrencies legal status. The policies and guidance related to the treatment of cryptocurrencies and information about any ongoing strategic efforts in the area is ongoing.

Types of Stakeholders

The legality of Bitcoin depends on who you are and what you're doing with it. There are three main categories of a Bitcoin stakeholders. Which are Users, Miners, and Exchanges. Some may fall under more than one of these categories, and each category has its own legal considerations.

Users

These are individuals that obtain Bitcoins, and either hodl them or spend them. Under the FinCEN guidance users who simply exchange Bitcoins for goods and services are using it legally.

FinCEN: A person that creates units of this convertible virtual currency and uses it to purchase real or virtual goods and services is a user of the convertible virtual currency and not subject to regulation as a money transmitter.

Miners

According to the FinCEN guidance, people creating bitcoins and exchanging them for fiat currency are not safe.

FinCEN: By contrast, a person that creates units of convertible virtual currency and sells those units to another person for real currency or its equivalent is engaged in transmission to another location and is a money transmitter.

Miners seem to fall into this category, which could theoretically make them liable for MTB classification. This is a bone of contention for bitcoin miners, who have asked for clarification.

This issue has not to our knowledge been tested in court.

Exchanges

Exchanges are a Money Transmitter Business (MTB).

What are the Legal Risks to Cryptocurrency Investors?

Along with the explosion of interest in digital currency and all of its implications for both new and traditional businesses, there is a growing need for clarity regarding the legal implications of these new technologies and currencies. As governments around the world, regulatory agencies, central banks, and other financial institutions are working to understand the nature and meaning of digital currencies, individual investors can make a great deal of money investing in this new space. On the other hand, investors assume certain legal risks when they buy and sell cryptocurrencies.

While digital currency might be easy to confuse for conventional electronic money, it is not the same; similarly, it is unlike conventional cash currencies because it cannot be physically owned and transferred between parties. Much of the murkiness of the legal standing of digital currency is because the space has only recently become popular as compared with more traditional currency and payment systems. Below, we'll explore some of the emerging legal implications associated with investing in cryptocurrencies.

Source: *https://www.investopedia.com/tech/what-are-legal-risks-cryptocurrency-investors/*

Cryptocurrencies as Property

One of the most critical legal considerations for any cryptocurrency investor has to do with the way that central authorities view cryptocurrency holdings. In the U.S., the IRS has defined cryptocurrencies as property, rather than as currencies proper. This means that individual investors are beholden to capital gains tax laws when it comes to reporting their cryptocurrency expenses and profits on their annual tax returns, regardless of where they purchased digital coins.

This aspect of the cryptocurrency space adds layers of confusion and complexity for U.S. taxpayers, but the difficulty does not end there. Indeed, it remains unclear whether digital currency investors who have purchased their holdings on foreign exchanges must face additional reporting measures come tax time. According to a report by CNBC, "anyone with more than $10,000 abroad usually needs to fill out the Report of Foreign Bank and Financial Accounts (FBAR)...with the Treasury Department each year. Another law--the Foreign Account Tax Compliance Act, or FATCA--requires certain U.S. taxpayers to describe their overseas accounts on Form 8938, when they file their taxes with the IRS."

Former federal tax prosecutor Kevin F. Sweeney offered a hint as to how foreign cryptocurrency exchanges could complicate tax matters for U.S. digital currency investors: "there probably is an FBAR requirement, but I wouldn't go as far as to say there always is one," he explained, adding that the lack of guidance from the IRS has created a "black hole" of uncertainty for investors and tax professionals alike. "It would seem awfully unfair if they would expect taxpayers to know that--and to then issue penalties for taxpayers who didn't do that--when practitioners can't even 100% figure out if there's an FBAR requirement," Sweeney added.

All of this suggests that digital currency investors should take special precautions to follow the advice of tax professionals when it comes to reporting cryptocurrency profits and losses. Because the rules are constantly changing, what may have been legally permissible last year or even months ago may now be cause for legal concern.

Source: *https://www.investopedia.com/tech/what-are-legal-risks-cryptocurrency-investors/*

Decentralized Status

One of the great draws of many digital currencies is also a potential risk factor for the individual investor. Bitcoin (BTC) has paved the way for other cryptocurrencies in that it is decentralized, meaning that it has no physical presence and is not backed by a central authority. While governments around the world have stepped in to assert their regulatory power in various ways, BTC and other digital currencies like it remain unattached to any jurisdiction or institution. On one hand, this frees investors from being beholden to those institutions. On the other hand, however, this status could result in legal complications. The value of digital currencies is dependent entirely upon the value that other owners and investors ascribe to them; this is true across all currencies, digital or fiat. Without a central authority backing the value of a digital currency, investors may be left in the lurch should complications with transactions or ownership arise.

Another potential risk associated with cryptocurrencies because of their decentralized status has to do with the particulars of transactions. In most other transactions, currency with a physical presence changes hand. In the case of electronic money, a trusted financial institution is involved in creating and settling deposits and debt claims. Neither of these concepts applies to cryptocurrency transactions. Because of this fundamental difference, legal confusion between parties in various types of digital currency transactions is a real possibility. Once again, because of the decentralized state of these currencies, the path of legal recourse in these situations can be difficult to assess.

Source: *https://www.investopedia.com/tech/what-are-legal-risks-cryptocurrency-investors/*

Business Registrations and Licensing

A growing number of businesses are taking advantage of digital currencies as a form of payment. As in other financial areas, businesses may be required to register and obtain licensure for jurisdictions and activities. Owing to the complex and evolving legal status of digital currencies, this area is significantly less clear for businesses operating in the crypto market. Companies which only accept cryptocurrencies, for example, may not need to register or obtain licenses at all. On the other hand, they may be required to submit to special considerations depending upon their jurisdiction. The onus of responsibility falls on business owners and managers to ensure that they are following proper legal procedure for their operations at both the local and state levels. At the federal level, for example, financial institutions must maintain certain activities related to protections against money laundering and fraud, transmission of funds, and more. Considerations like these also apply to businesses dealing with digital currencies.

Source: *https://www.investopedia.com/tech/what-are-legal-risks-cryptocurrency-investors/*

Fraud and Money Laundering

There is a widespread belief that cryptocurrencies provide criminal organizations with a new means of committing fraud, money laundering, and a host of other financial crimes.

This may not directly impact most cryptocurrency investors who do not intend to use this new technology to commit such crimes. However, investors who find themselves in the unfortunate position of being a victim of financial crime do not likely have the same legal options as traditional victims of fraud.

This issue also relates to the decentralized status of digital currencies. When a cryptocurrency exchange is hacked and customers' holdings are stolen, for instance, there is frequently no standard practice for recovering the missing funds. Digital currency investors thus take on a certain amount of risk by purchasing and holding cryptocurrency assets. It is for this reason that developers and startups related to digital currency have focused such a great deal of attention on creating secure means of holding digital coins and tokens. Still, while new types of wallets are being released all the time, and while cryptocurrency exchanges are always improving their security measures, investors have so far not been able to fully eliminate the legal risks associated with owning cryptocurrencies, and it's likely that they never will.

Source: *https://www.investopedia.com/tech/what-are-legal-risks-cryptocurrency-investors/*

What Is A 51 Percent Attack?

A **51%** attack on a **blockchain** refers to a miner or a group of miners trying to control more than 50% of a network's mining power, computing power or hash rate. People in control of such mining power can block new transactions from taking place or being confirmed.

How To Keep Bitcoins Safe

If you are thinking through the process of accruing bitcoins, you may be wondering where to keep them once you've done so. After investing time and resources into the digital asset, can you be sure they are locked safely away for when you want to use them?

Bitcoins aren't "stored" anywhere. They are accessible through Bitcoin addresses, which require a set of digital keys for entry. So, the question of how to securely store Bitcoins comes down to the security of these keys. Every Bitcoin address has two keys: a "public key" and a "private key." Bitcoin addresses are derived from public keys, and these Bitcoin addresses are shared.

A private key is what allows users to take Bitcoins from a wallet or to send them to others, and it is what must be protected to keep a user's bitcoins safe. Whoever holds the private key is considered to be the "owner" of the Bitcoins at that address, although technically it's possible to possess somebody else's keys without owning the bitcoins they lead to. There are a few different methods that users employ for protecting their private keys.

To hold a private key, it's possible to encrypt bitcoin wallets with a private password, but this is generally the most basic level of security and one that could potentially be breached by computer hackers or viruses. Others opt to keep their access offline completely. Instead, they hold private keys in disconnected databases so that they remain safe from threats on the internet.

How Bitcoin Mining Works

In traditional fiat money systems, governments simply print more money when they need to. But in Bitcoin computers around the world they 'mine' for coins by competing with each other.

How Does Mining Take Place?

People are sending Bitcoins to each other over the bitcoin network all the time, but unless someone keeps a record of all these transactions, no-one would be able to keep track of who had paid what. The bitcoin network deals with this by collecting all of the transactions made during a set period into a list, called a block. It's the miners' job to confirm those transactions, and write them into a general ledger.

This general ledger is a long list of blocks, known as the 'blockchain'. It can be used to explore any transaction made between any Bitcoin addresses, at any point on the network. Whenever a new block of transactions is created, it is added to the blockchain, creating an increasingly lengthy list of all the transactions that ever took place on the bitcoin network. A constantly updated copy of the block is given to everyone who participates, so that they know what is going on.

But a general ledger has to be trusted, and all of this is held digitally. How can we be sure that the blockchain stays intact, and is never tampered with? This is where the miners come in.

When a block of transactions is created, miners put it through a process. They take the information in the block, and apply a mathematical formula to it, turning it into something else.

That something else is a far shorter, seemingly random sequence of letters and numbers known as a hash. This hash is stored along with the block, at the end of the blockchain at that point in time.

Hashes have some interesting properties. It's easy to produce a hash from a collection of data like a bitcoin block, but it's practically impossible to work out what the data was just by looking at the hash. And while it is very easy to produce a hash from a large amount of data, each hash is unique. If you change just one character in a bitcoin block, its hash will change completely.

Miners don't just use the transactions in a block to generate a hash. Some other pieces of data are used too. One of these pieces of data is the hash of the last block stored in the blockchain.

Because each block's hash is produced using the hash of the block before it, it becomes a digital version of a wax seal. It confirms that this block – and every block after it – is legitimate, because if you tampered with it, everyone would know.

If you tried to fake a transaction by changing a block that had already been stored in the blockchain, that block's hash would change. If someone checked the block's authenticity by running the hashing function on it, they'd find that the hash was different from the one already stored along with that block in the blockchain. The block would be instantly spotted as a fake.

Because each block's hash is used to help produce the hash of the next block in the chain, tampering with a block would also make the subsequent block's hash wrong too. That would continue all the way down the chain, throwing everything out of whack.

Competing for Coins

So, that's how miners 'seal off' a block. They all compete with each other to do this, using software written specifically to mine blocks. Every time someone successfully creates a hash, they get a reward of 25 bitcoins, the blockchain is updated, and everyone on the network hears about it. That's the incentive to keep mining, and keep the transactions working.

The problem is that it's very easy to produce a hash from a collection of data. Computers are really good at this. The bitcoin network has to make it more difficult, otherwise everyone would be hashing hundreds of transaction blocks each second, and all of the Bitcoins would be mined in minutes. The bitcoin protocol deliberately makes it more difficult, by introducing something called 'proof of work'.

The bitcoin protocol won't just accept any old hash. It demands that a block's hash has to look a certain way; it must have a certain number of zeroes at the start. There's no way of telling what a hash is going to look like before you produce it, and as soon as you include a new piece of data in the mix, the hash will be totally different.

Miners aren't supposed to meddle with the transaction data in a block, but they must change the data they're using to create a different hash. They do this using another, random piece of data called a 'nonce'. This is used with the transaction data to create a hash. If the hash doesn't fit the required format, the nonce is changed, and the whole thing is hashed again. It can take many attempts to find a nonce that works, and all the miners in the network are trying to do it at the same time. That's how miners earn their bitcoins.

Is Bitcoin Mining Profitable?

The bitcoin network is a perfectly balanced set of participants, where nobody trusts anybody else but everybody is incentivized to play their part, verifying everything. Bitcoin miners provide the security that gives Bitcoins value, and in return they are paid with a combination of newly issued currency and the network fees that people pay to use the Bitcoin network. The Bitcoin network adjusts how difficult it is to mine Bitcoin every two weeks, and so far there are no indications of any shortage of miners!

Where Is Bitcoin Accepted?

Bitcoin and other cryptocurrencies are relishing in newfound media coverage. Between the sheer outperformance of these digital currencies compared to the broader stock market, to recent ransomware attacks (e.g., WannaCry) where the perpetrators demand payment in Bitcoin in order to "unlock" a computer, bitcoin is in the spotlight.

The more media coverage it receives, the more interest there will likely be in this burgeoning payment and investment platform.

Weakness in the world's most prominent currency, the U.S. dollar, may be helping as well. President Trump has, on numerous occasions, proclaimed the U.S. dollar to be too strong. A weaker dollar can help promote the export of American goods, but U.S. consumers aren't typically huge fans of seeing their currency weakened.

Some investors have used the dollar's weakness as an opportunity to invest in bitcoin, which is a "finite" resource since the maximum number of Bitcoin is limited to 21 million. The fact that the dollar's monetary base can be expanded infinitely and bitcoin is limited provides the belief to some investors that bitcoin could be a better means to preserve and grow wealth over time.

Bitcoin has also benefited from a growing acceptance of the currency by countries, industries, and businesses. Japan declared the cryptocurrency legal tender earlier this year, while some retailers within the marijuana industry have been using Bitcoin as a bridge currency between bank-issued debit and credit cards and marijuana product purchases.

Since marijuana is a federally illegal substance, most banks won't deal with pot-based businesses, so bitcoin services act as an intermediary by allowing consumers to buy Bitcoin and pay for their pot products that way. Bitcoin services then transfer that bitcoin back to cash for the marijuana business in return for a nominal service charge.

Alternative Cryptocurrency

There are hundreds of alternative cryptocurrencies. See Top 30 Cryptocurrency Names, Acronyms and Symbols at the end of the book.

Some of the top alternative cryptocurrencies are:

Ethereum

After bitcoin, Ethereum is the second largest player in the cryptocurrency space that's changing how we handle money, with over 30 percent market share. Unlike Bitcoin, Ether wasn't built with the intention of being a currency for everyday use. Instead, it is used by application developers as a currency for transactions on the Ethereum network, which includes a range of applications like ride-sharing, betting and investment.

Ripple XRP

Ripple XRP was designed to allow banks to quickly and easily transfer funds between various existing currencies. XRP has a big advantage over bitcoin, as it can currently process over 1,000 transactions per second, whereas bitcoin is limited to seven per second. One reason to consider investing in XRP:

Litecoin

Litecoin uses similar programming to bitcoin, but with a few technical modifications that make it more accessible for general use.

Zcash

Zcash claims to be a more secure version of bitcoin that uses upgraded blockchain technology.

Dash

Dash, formerly known as Darkcoin, is another cryptocurrency that has seen a rise in interest as Bitcoin has become more popular. Dash recently formed partnerships with a gift card operator and payments gateway.

SECTION 2: CRYPTOCURRENCY

What Is a Cryptocurrency?

A cryptocurrency is a digital or virtual currency that is secured by cryptography, which makes it nearly impossible to counterfeit or double-spend. Many cryptocurrencies are decentralized networks based on blockchain technology—a distributed ledger enforced by a disparate network of computers. A defining feature of cryptocurrencies is that they are generally not issued by any central authority, rendering them theoretically immune to government interference or manipulation.

KEY TAKEAWAYS

1. A cryptocurrency is a new form of digital asset based on a network that is distributed across a large number of computers. This decentralized structure allows them to exist outside the control of governments and central authorities.
2. The word "cryptocurrency" is derived from the encryption techniques which are used to secure the network.
3. Blockchains, which are organizational methods for ensuring the integrity of transactional data, is an essential component of many cryptocurrencies.
4. Many experts believe that blockchain and related technology will disrupt many industries, including finance and law.
5. Cryptocurrencies face criticism for a number of reasons, including their use for illegal activities, exchange rate volatility, and vulnerabilities of the

infrastructure underlying them. However, they also have been praised for their portability, divisibility, inflation resistance, and transparency.

Source:
https://www.investopedia.com/terms/c/cryptocurrency.asp

Understanding Cryptocurrencies

Cryptocurrencies are systems that allow for the secure payments online which are denominated in terms of virtual "tokens," which are represented by ledger entries internal to the system. "Crypto" refers to the various encryption algorithms and cryptographic techniques that safeguard these entries, such as elliptical curve encryption, public-private key pairs, and hashing functions.

Source:
https://www.investopedia.com/terms/c/cryptocurrency.asp

Types of Cryptocurrency

The first blockchain-based cryptocurrency was Bitcoin, which still remains the most popular and most valuable. Today, there are thousands of alternate cryptocurrencies with various functions and specifications. Some of these are clones or forks of Bitcoin, while others are new currencies that were built from scratch.

Source:
https://www.investopedia.com/terms/c/cryptocurrency.asp

SECTION 3: BLOCKCHAINS

Blockchains are digital ledgers and can be formally defined as a continuously-growing list of records that are linked tougher and secured using advanced cryptography. In more simple terms, a blockchain is literally a chain of blocks. Each record in the list of a blockchain's chain is called a block that contains specific types and pieces of information. Each block will usually include some sort of pointer as a link to the previous bock, transaction data, and a timestamp, which can take a variety of forms.

Another way to look at is that a blockchain is much like a database where each entry is linked to the previous and next entry. This means that the information contained within the blockchain can't be changed, once a block with specific data is added to the chain. Depending on the chain that you are looking at, there are often useful tools for exploring that will allow you to scan the transaction data.

Blockchains are resistant to being modified because of their inherent design. This allows blockchains to record transactions between different parties efficiently. These transactions are not only verifiable but permanent as well. Once information is recorded in a blockchain, the data cannot be altered after-the-fact without altering the subsequent blocks by having the majority of nodes on the network agreeing to the change.

This inability to change the data within a blockchain make illegal or unfair actions almost impossible to carry out. If a hacker wished to alter information within a blockchain, they would have to gain control of every node. This security is one of the most useful characteristics of the blockchain.

Since blockchains are designed to be verifiable and permanent, they are especially suitable for recording events, maintaining medical records, drawing up agreements, fundraising, and keeping track of other documents.

Blockchain Basics

Whether you are aware of it or not, you conduct business every day, even if you don't work. At some point, everyone gets online and initiates some kind of transaction. Whether it is purchasing something from Amazon or buying something from iTunes, you are engaging in the business of blockchain technology.

Even though the term "blockchain" is relatively new, the technology has been around for about a decade. The digitized ledger that Satoshi Nakamoto created in 2008 was the basis for the spreadsheets that manage cryptocurrencies and other online trading transactions. The technology is used in cryptography, which is how text is coded on the Internet.

Cryptography is used in blockchain technology to create distributed trust networks. This, in turn, allows any contributor to the system to operate the transactions securely without having to obtain authorization from someone else in the digital ledger. These transactions are then verified, approved, and then recorded in an encrypted block. This block is saved intermittently and then connected to the previous block, which in turn creates a chain.

Components of a Blockchain

Two main parts make up a blockchain. The first component is the decentralized network. The decentralized network is what facilitates and verifies the transactions that are made. Having blockchains on a decentralized network means that the software isn't limited to one computer system. Instead, it can be controlled on multiple computer systems, and more importantly, it isn't controlled by the government.

The second component is the indisputable ledger where the transactions are processed and recorded in a location that is secure. This security makes it almost impossible for someone who is not connected to the chain to make changes or steal information.

Since there can be numerous contributors involved in any blockchain, any of the contributors can control the information that is entered into the ledger. Since every transaction is processed securely, and given a permanent time-stamp, it can become challenging for another contributor to alter the ledger in any way.

Blockchain technology can be used for various computerized and internet-based application. One of these applications is smartcontracts. Smart contracts allow businesses to automatically verify and execute agreements that function independently in a secure environment. Blockchain technology acts as a middleman for implementing all business deals, protocols, and programmed exchanges of information in smart contracts. As more and more transactions are completed online, to not only run our personal lives but professional lives as well, more and more deals are being signed and created online.

Blockchain applications have begun to become increasingly popular in the medical field in recent years. Researchers are now investigating these applications dealing with digital identity, insurance records, and medical records. There are many medical offices today that use some kind of digital machine to verify that the information they have on file is, in fact, your information.

Security Concerns

One of the most significant issues people are faced with today is the thought that all their information could be compromised by hackers because most of our personal information is digitized. It also seems that it has become too easy for complete strangers to access, copy and tamper with our data. However, it is still a risk that we all take despite the increasing probability of being hacked. Blockchain technology was created to help ensure that doesn't happen or in the very least make it more challenging to try.

For someone to hack the blockchain system, they would need to go back and change every single block. That would require a ton of effort and patience because blockchains could have upwards of billions of chains linked that a person would have to go through and change. Changing just one or two blocks would automatically send an alert that the system is being hacked. This is only one of the many reasons why blockchain technology has become so popular.

Blockchain technology can be used for a variety of other things as well. It can also be used for global payments, sharing music, or tracking diamond sales.

Types of Blockchain

There are three major types of blockchain. There are private blockchains, public blockchains, and consortium blockchains.

Public blockchains are created by the public. Anyone can participate in the creation, confirmation, and recordation of the content that is put into the blockchain. There isn't just one person in charge of overseeing the transactions that happen in this kind of blockchain.

Because there isn't a single person in charge of these blockchains, decisions are made by many decentralized agreement tools such as proof of work, which a computer algorithm that is used by cryptocurrencies like Bitcoin. Public blockchains are open and crystal clear in content, making it easy for anyone who looks at them to understand what they are and what they can do.

Public blockchains are privately owned by an individual or organization. With public blockchains, there is a single, designated person in charge. While there can be several contributors to this type of blockchain, the final transactions are either approved or disapproved by the person in charge and then recorded.

The purpose of **consortium blockchains**, also known as **federated blockchains**, is to remove the only autonomy given to just one contributor by the use of private blockchains. This type of blockchain allows for more than one contributor to be in charge. Instead, there is a group of companies or individuals that gather and make decisions that benefit the entire network.

Blockchain Technology

Blockchain technology is an irreversible, encrypted, decentralized ledger that has the potential to make all centralized activities, processes, and organizations entirely autonomous. This means that a person will have the ability to eliminate the middleman and specialists, effectively reforming every single business in the world.

Blockchain technology is merely a way to keep track of any money or trading exchanges you engage in online. You can think of it like an accountant who keeps track of all the money that you spend. Currently, blockchain technology is mostly used to handle any type of situation that deals with cryptocurrency, like Bitcoin. Let's consider the following example.

When you complete a transaction using Bitcoin, that specific transaction is processed through the blockchain. Before the transaction can be achieved, you or someone connected to your Bitcoin account has to verify that the transaction is legitimate. Once the transaction can be confirmed as being valid, it is recorded and saved to a ledger that is controlled by the blockchain. At this point, nobody can change or alter the transaction in any way. Only you or those with access to your account can verify transactions.

Blockchain technology is controlled by a decentralized network, which means that it isn't controlled by any government. By running on a decentralized system, it is much easier to conduct business transactions. It is also more private because you don't have a federal bank holding your money or other assets. Everything is strictly handled by you and your company. To understand the importance of decentralization, you need to consider the following examples of centralization and decentralization.

Centralization

When you use your debit card at the bookstore, you swipe your card to pay for your purchases. At this point, the company then sends a bill to your bank for the amount agreed to when you paid for your goods. The bank then must verify that it was you who made the purchase. The bank, once the transaction is confirmed, releases the money to the company and records the transaction in their ledger. The ledger the bank recorded the transaction in, includes all the operations the bank made on behalf of the card you used. The bank has complete control over what happens with the ledger. Other than having the ability to look at your banking statements, you have no authority to change anything or do anything with the ledger. Centralized ledgers are much easier to hack because they are controlled by multiple entities.

Decentralized

Imagine that you want to transfer 1.00 Bitcoin to someone. All you have to do is tell whoever is in charge of the network, whether it's one person or a group of people, that you are transferring 1.00 Bitcoin. Once this is done, the transaction is approved and then it is recorded.

Decentralized blockchains are much better than centralized transactions because it takes less time to complete a single transaction. Other reasons decentralized blockchains are better is that a person or company can send secure information to another person or company, such as encrypted messages and medical records.

The Business of Blockchain

Everybody has trust issues with something in their lives. Many people today, don't trust inputting their information into the internet. However, even with this mistrust, it hasn't stopped many people from continuing to do it.

One purpose of blockchain technology is to help ease the distrust that people have with inputting their information on the internet and is one of the main reasons why companies are increasingly investing their money in the use of this technology. In fact, between 2013 and 2016, a study showed that blockchainmanaged funds reached a total of $1.6 billion, which equates to a 1,600 percent increase.

Industries that Use Blockchain Technology

The financial industry is one of the sectors that have greatly benefitted from the use of blockchain technology. This is because of the vast sums of money and transactions that are in play in the industry. Here are a couple of examples of the different companies that are utilizing blockchain technology today.

Crowdlending

Crowdlending campaigns have started to take over the act of having to go to the bank to get a loan. Crowdlending is a person to person lending company. Today, there are, on average, more than 50 billion person to person loans being made worldwide. This industry will likely feel an enormous boost with the use of blockchain technology.

IBM Global Financing Unit

IBM has become one of the major players in blockchain technology use, with a proven track record of being a great asset for tracing transactions. IBM's Global Financing Unit processes $2.9 million in payables for the company every year. It is also responsible for granting credit to more than four thousand suppliers. IBM has been successful in lowering dispute settlements by 25 percent, thanks in part to blockchain technology. This decrease in percentage has resulted in the group being able to free up $100 million in pre-confirmed capital for other purposes.

Bookkeeping Industry

The bookkeeping industry has greatly benefited from blockchain technology. Every transaction that takes place in the economy today is registered internally in the private records of individual market participants. Blockchain technology takes place when accounting expands past the borders of the network.

Value Added

There are numerous ways that blockchain technology can add value to a business. One way is by building a network for your business. Dr. Michael Yuan, the Chief Scientist of CyberMiles notes how blockchain can provide value to startups and companies. His theory is that the key benefit of blockchains will deliver the ability to construct a network for all kinds of businesses. What his theory states are that rather than competing against each other, companies can collaborate and build a system with each business industry having its own chain.

Another way that blockchain technology can add value to a business is by banking the unbanked. It might be hard to believe, but there are a lot of people in the world who don't have bank accounts. Blockchain technology will provide the opportunity for these people to create a bank account. Someone could just open a Bitcoin account and in return have a digital wallet.

A third way in which blockchain technology can add value to a business is by lowering the time for transactions to be complete. Again, time is playing a significant role in the blockchain world. Christopher Brown, CEO of Modular, create Blossom, a digital wallet for Ethereum. The program is a multi-featured desktop wallet application that gives businesses and users a more straightforward way to handle their funds. It takes less time than if you were to head to the bank to get cash.

Next, blockchain technology can add value to businesses through legal contracts. This can be done by linking the Internet of Things (IoT) data and blockchain technology. Utilizing the data from IoT devices allows individuals and businesses to connect to legal contracts that have been saved on the blockchain. For example, when you are buying a house, all the documents that you sign, must also be signed by the seller. This means that all the documents must be in one place for both parties to have access. Outside information from IoT connected devices is linked to the blockchain, making the legal contracts immediately usable without anyone being able to interfere in the process.

Monetization

The final way that blockchain technology can add value to a business is by helping with monetization. The ways companies are making money are changing. People no longer pay attention to ads because you can now fast-forward through the commercials and online they can be ignored. Plus, the money generally goes to the site where the ad is placed, which has a tremendous impact on business.

Blockchain technology solves this problem. This is because every part of the content that is created for ads is recorded on

45

the blockchain, which is how content creators are rewarded through cryptocurrency or fiat currency.

Growing Money

Many experts believe that blockchain technology will become the way of the future. Cryptocurrency is rapidly increasing because people want to put their money in a place that is not only safe and secure, but that will also gain value like a savings account. However, savings accounts aren't as secure as they would like. By the end of 2017, future markets had already been created for Bitcoin. That was also the year the finance industry saw a dramatic increase in Initial Coin Offerings, (ICO). In the last year,

ICOs have gained more money than venture capital investments.

While cryptocurrencies continue to improve in their abilities to quickly process transactions, eventually they will compete against credit card companies processing of transactions.

The Cloud and Blockchain

At some point, everyone has used the cloud to back up data that they don't want to lose. If you didn't know, the cloud actually runs on a blockchain. Experts say that we have started to take luxury for granted. In the past, you couldn't merely click a button and automatically save data to a backup site like iCloud or OneDrive. Instead, you were required to transfer the information on a compact disk or flash drive. Then, you would have to take the disk or flash drive to another computer to download the data.

While you can still do this today, there isn't a guarantee that this type of technology will last. Like the floppy disks of the past, compact discs and flash drives may become obsolete, but internet saving applications will always be updated because we now live in a tech-savvy world.

Blockchain and Gaming

eSports and online fantasy sports have grown significantly over the last decade with more and more people creating online fantasy sports teams. Online games, like Fantasy Football, were some of the first sites to adopt the earliest versions of Bitcoin and other cryptocurrencies. They also use blockchain technology to run and keep up with the gaming technology.

The uses of blockchain technology don't just stop with fantasy sports. The most popular smartphone applications to download today are games. This is why, as the technology grows, more developers will likely make use of blockchains, as well as cryptocurrencies.

Supply Chain Management and Blockchain

Blockchain technology will also benefit supply chain management by providing a way to trace goods while at the same time being cost effective. For example, sending packages through the United Parcel Services from one business to another. In the past, someone had to call to find out where their box was if it hadn't arrived when it was supposed to. Today, you are provided with a tracking number that allows you to see where the package you sent or are waiting for is in transit, which creates a blockchain.

Blockchain technology has made it easier for businesses to do business together because it has dramatically simplified the production process, and transfer process, as well as the verification and payment methods, used.

Blockchain Technology and Quality Assurance

In business, mistakes happen, no matter how careful you are and how closely you follow processes and procedures, and it can be challenging to pin down how the mistake occurred. With blockchain technology, mistakes and errors can be traced back to the point of origin. Not only does this make it easier to investigate mistakes, but it also saves companies time and money.

Proof of Work Vs. Proof of Stake

A majority of the public blockchains that are currently available are based on a proof of work system. However, in 2018, the second biggest cryptocurrency, Ethereum, began testing a new system that would change its blockchain from a proof of work to a proof of state system. Before we can get into what exactly this means, it is essential to understand what exactly is occurring when a transaction is verified.

Proof of Work

The mining of Bitcoin is accomplished by using a high-powered machine that will utilize a SHA256 double round has a verification process with the purpose of validating Bitcoin transactions as they happen. This is done to provide security for the sanctity of the Bitcoin blockchain. The speed that your machine can mine Bitcoins is measured regarding hashes per second.

Bitcoin, in exchange for this service, compensates those that are doing the mining by offering them a fraction of a Bitcoin for every validation. They do this to offset time and energy costs. Additionally, those who initiate the transaction will typically provide some amount of a transaction fee to help offset costs as well. The higher the computer processing power of your Bitcoin mining machine, the more you can make through the process.

To be accepted into the blockchain, each block must have a valid proof of work. A proof of work is a type of data that is both difficult to produce as well as time-consuming. Creating proof of work is essentially a random process with a low probability of success. This means that a Bitcoin mining machine that is trying to complete the process requires a significant degree of trial and error to be successful. Bitcoin uses what is known as the hashcash proof of work.

The hashcash proof of work is a type of cryptographic algorithm that makes use of a hash function as a core building block of the mining process. The most common hashcash function that is used today is the haschash-Sha256. This particular proof of work function was created by Dr. Adam Back in the 1990s. It was initially used as a way to prevent email spam abuse because successfully generating the hashcash for a single email was simple. However, creating one for a vast number of emails at the same time proved to be much more difficult.

You can tweak hashcash proofs of work for the difficulty to ensure that new blocks aren't being generated faster than the network can handle. This means that a new block can't be generated more than once every ten minutes at this time. As the probability of each successive generation is low, this makes it challenging to determine which Bitcoin machine is going to generate the next block.

For a new block to be considered valid, its hash value must end up being less than that of the current target. This means that each block will have to naturally indicate that work has been completed to generate it. Each block also contains the hash of the preceding block, which is how the chain understands where each block falls within the overall blockchain. To change a block, the work must be redone on all the previous blocks, and new and connected hashes must be generated for all of them. The blockchain is then essentially protected from tampering, because of the enormous computational power that is needed.

Proof of Stake

Most of the significant cryptocurrencies today work off of some variation of the proof of work model, either through the SHA256 hash or through another, similar hash. However, Ethereum, Bitcoin's largest competitor, has been working on an alternative that could significantly change the way blockchain transactions are verified.

In early 2017, Ethereum released the implementation guide for a hybrid proof of work/proof of stake system. They are rolling out this new system in phases before they make it the platform's primary verification system. The plan currently states that the blockchain platform will alternate between the two systems. With the new system, about one out of every 100 blocks will use the new system while the rest will continue to use the old system.

There hope is that the new system will improve the rate at which they can produce new blocks. This will mark the first step in the plans for Ethereum's evolution. This will be the first time a proof of stake system will be used to secure a blockchain, which will be a significant step forward. This new system will serve as the proof of concept test for an alternative to the proof of work model that dominates the cryptocurrency today and provide proponents the ability to test their claim of its superiority. When the new proof of stake model is rolled out on a larger scale, it will significantly reduce the amount of electricity that is required to verify a single block.

It's important to understand just how the proof of stake system differs from the proof of work model. With proof of stake verification, rather than having the miner solve the equation to verify the block, a validator, who is confirmed reliable by the stake they have in the system, will commit to its accuracy. They know that if they lie, they will lose their own ether as well.

During the first stage of deployment, all of the blocks that are verified through the new system will also be checked through the old system to help double verify that the blocks contain the information that they should, while also testing the accuracy of the new system. Validators will then look at the various chains that are available and make a decision based on how much ether is currently in the chain. If they make a poor choice, they will lose their money. This process will help form a consensus that leads to a single more massive chain from the many smaller ones.

Benefits of the Proof of Stake Model

While the process of implementing the proof of stake model isn't smooth sailing, it doesn't mean that the proof of stake system is going to lose out. It contains many clear benefits over the more traditional process. This first clear benefit that this new model will have is that it will drop the more than one million dollars Ethereum miners spend on electricity each day to around $100,000 or just ten percent.

In addition to making it cheaper to mine cryptocurrency, the proof of stake model will also make it more unrestricted because it won't matter how fast the user's computer is because the calculations will be completed within the blockchain itself. As a bonus, this makes the 51 percent attack much more difficult to pull off successfully. A 51 percent attack happens when a group of miners comes together to control more than 51 percent of all nodes running a particular blockchain in an attempt to add completely false blocks to the system that the unaffected nodes will then accept as accurate because a majority of the nodes are already reporting it that way.

Proof of stake will also make it possible to ensure the validators stay honest by forcing them to be vested in the transactions that they verify because they know if they don't play fair, they will lose their own money. Finally, the proof of stake model makes it easier to produce blocks faster than ever thanks to a process called sharding, which is the process of breaking a more extensive database down into more manageable pieces. When databases are broken down, it allows each piece to have its own set of validators who complete their own transactions within the shard. Once this occurs, it makes scalability more modular and even faster.

Proof of Stake Challenges

The new process won't be without its own share of issues. The first issue will be that the new system isn't guaranteed to work. This is because this type of model hasn't been put into play at a large scale before. This means that there is a chance that the original blockchain could be damaged if the transactions aren't processed as planned, or if a smart contract is miswritten. To combat this scenario, the Ethereum team is working on what is called the finality property. This will ensure that the current state of the blockchain will be secure before the new one can be implemented.

Benefits of Blockchain Technology

The promise of blockchain technology saw all of the world's contracts and agreements digitized into code and stored in public, transparent databases that are safe from being deleted, tampered with, or revised. The future will see every kind of agreement, business process, online task, funds payment, and transactions with a single digital record that can be identified and validated. As the technology continues to expand, we'll see middlemen, like lawyers, stock exchange brokers, and banks, saving billions, if not trillions of dollars every year.

Blockchain technology is ideally suited to revolutionizing the way many industries do business. Here are just some of the ways that blockchain technology will accomplish this.

Eliminating Third Parties

Blockchain technology will eradicate third parties and increase the number of exchanges that aren't subject to trust issues.

Blockchain will allow two or more parties to conduct a transaction, of any type, without having to resort to official oversight or intermediation with an external party. This will significantly reduce, or even eliminate counterparty risks.

Counterparty risk is a risk that each party of a contract will face if the counterparty doesn't live up to their contractual obligations. It is a risk to both parties and is something that should always be considered when evaluating a contract.

Control Over Data

With blockchain, users are more empowered and have better control over their own data. With blockchain protocols in place, users own and are in control of all their information and transactions themselves. Uber is a perfect example of this. Uber is one of the world's largest car services companies, but they don't actually own any of the cars that run its business, but they rake in billions of dollars through car rides that are logged by drivers using the Uber app.

Better Data Quality and Integrity

With the blockchain technology, data is always complete because the next block can't be created or mined without being linked to a verified block being finished in the chain. It is also consistent because all the data has to conform to the protocol standards or else it won't be recorded in the chain, as well as being widely available.

Durability and Reliability

Blockchain technology has been proven not to have a single point of failure and is capable of withstanding malicious exterior attacks more efficiently. This is compared to closed systems that contain possible weaknesses and point of failure that are scattered throughout the entire system from within.

The Integrity of Data Processing and Transfers

Due to the unchangeable nature of the blocks in a blockchain, every user on the network can trust that every transaction they make will take place on the network and that they will always be executed precisely as the system was designed. This removes the need for any third party to oversee the transactions, maintaining the integrity of the data being processed and all transfers.

Transparency and Auditability

All transactions made to and on a blockchain are, by design, created on a public ledger that can be looked at by everyone. This creates a highly transparent system that can be searched by anyone. There are various services, such as etherscan.io, that allows users to search the vast databases and transactions in order to audit everything that is happening within and on a blockchain.

Faster Transactions

Transactions between banks, like ACH, (automated clearinghouse transactions) can take days to clear. This is especially true for transactions that are made outside of regular working hours. Just think about when you send a wire or make a purchase at the end of the business day on Friday. Without blockchains, you are unable to see any timely updates to the status of your funds. Often you aren't provided an update until the following Tuesday or Wednesday.

Blockchain technology reduces the transaction times to minutes, and sometimes even seconds, and they are processed around the clock.

Lower Transaction Costs

With blockchains, no outside parties are overlooking the transactions. Because of this blockchains can potentially reduce the transaction fees significantly. With reduced transaction fees, it could possibly lead to billions of dollars being saved annually.

RISKS AND CHALLENGES OF BLOCKCHAIN TECHNOLOGY

One of the major draws of blockchain technology is also one of its most significant challenges. Currently, there is very little regulation with regards to what is and isn't allowed in the blockchain space. Because of this, there have been numerous instances of hackers being able to make off with millions of dollars of investor money because of loopholes in the online blockchain systems. Despite the promise of security on the current blockchains, there are teething issues that hackers are taking advantage of to the detriment of every blockchain user.

Recently, there was a case with Enigma, a decentralized platform that was preparing to raise money through an ICO. Hackers were able to hack Enigma's website and numerous social accounts successfully. This allowed the hackers to send out spam to Enigma's community and make off with almost $500,000. The Enigma project was launched by a group of MIT graduates, who sent out invites for people to join the Enigma community. The hackers grabbed money from those who joined the company's official mailing list and Slack group. In all, there were around 9,000 users and participants who were affected by this security breach.

The hacker's effectively posted messages on Slack altered the official website and spoofed emails to the community list to make it look like the company was making a formal request for money. Members of the community responded by sending money that was deposited directly into the hacker's crypto wallet.

Last year there was a similar hack but on a much larger scale. When the Decentralized Autonomous Organization or DAO that was built on Ethereum was hacked and resulted in a loss of $50 million to hackers.

The DAO was supposed to be a decentralized investment fund where decisions wouldn't rest on just a few partners, but rather anyone who invested in the fund would have a vote in which companies or projects the company should invest in. It was set up so that the more that you contributed, the more votes you got.

Since the fund was built to be distributed, no one could take the money and run. Unfortunately, due to human error and programming errors, hackers were able to exploit the system to receive a $50 million payday, which has of yet been recovered.

Another example of the challenges facing blockchain technology comes from a company called OneCoin. Recently, a company known as Gnosis sold $12..5 million worth of a token called GNO in just over ten minutes. The sale was intended to pay for the development of an advanced prediction market. The initial coin offering, ICO, received rave reviews across the global press.

On that same day, a company called OneCoin, based in Mumbai, India, was in the middle of a sales pitch for its own digital currency when their offices were raided by financial enforcement officers. In the end, eighteen OneCoin reps were jailed, and more than $2 million in investor funds were seized. Multiple authorities describe OneCoin, which was being touted as the next Bitcoin, as a Ponzi scheme. By the time the offices in Mumbai were raided, the company had already moved at least $350 million in scammed funds.

Since there are no checks and balances to govern the execution of ICOs, if you are going to invest in a coin, you need to ensure that you aren't investing in any random idea that could turn out to be a scam.

Major Hurdles of Blockchain

Currently, there are significant hurdles in the way of formally legalizing and regulating crypto trades. Similar challenges exist with market growth and adoption. Some of the issues surrounding blockchain include, what kinds of tax structures are right for blockchain markets, how to trace and aggregate funds, and where will spending and income information come from and how it will be gathered. As long as these problems remain question marks on the policy boards of decision makers, widespread adoption of blockchain technology will be difficult.

However, there is some promise for the future of blockchain technology. South Korea and Japan have made significant advances recently that will allow for legal Bitcoin transactions, and various applications have opened investment channels in the blockchain space to traditional investors. These advancements have led to an influx of funds to different blockchain companies, which, in turn, have been able to invest in growth, research, and the promotion of their particular blockchain services.

Risks of Blockchain Technology

As a new technology, resolving challenges like transaction speed, the verification process, and data limits are standing in the way of making blockchain widely adopted technology. The regulatory status of blockchain projects is also a risk of blockchain technology and is currently uncertain.

If financial institutions and governments don't buy into the idea of blockchain technology, or if it is pushed away because of a lack of clear guidelines on how the industry should be regulated, blockchain will never gain the widespread adoption that investors and experts are hoping for, leaving it to be a novelty idea and nothing more.

The mining of blocks is highly energy intensive and is becoming even more expensive with the creation of each new block on the chain. There may end up being a limit to how much miners are willing to continue to spend to solve mathematical puzzles in order to earn a few Bitcoins as their reward.

There are also cybersecurity and integration concerns that will have to be addressed before the general public will be willing to entrust their personal data to a blockchain solution. This also goes for getting the go-ahead from any body of users or a Board of Directors in order to make significant changes to or even completely replacing an existing system.

Finally, there is the problem of social and cultural adoption of blockchain technology. Blockchain represents a complete shift to a decentralized network. This requires a significant buy-in of all users and operators on the network. Also, since it is such a significant development, it is not entirely understood by a majority of the population. Will all of these risks and hurdles, it may be several years before we see widespread adoption of blockchain solutions.

Is Blockchain Technology Right For You

The most common reasons that someone might consider an experiment with blockchain is a continuous desire to experiment with new technologies, a need for blockchain's timestamp technology or an interest in the many different ways blockchain can safeguard existing data. As with any new technology, it is essential that you look before you leap and consider if blockchain technology is really right for you and your business.

Know Who Will Be Looking at Your Data

In a majority of the traditional centralized databases, anyone with access to it has their activities stored in case they need to be reviewed later. If you need to have many individuals look at your data on a regular basis, but don't want them to have write access to the data, then you may benefit from using a blockchain. Utilizing a blockchain in your business may help to streamline the process by providing users with read-only access in addition to a having a log in a more traditional sense when it is required.

Writeable Data

An average user database is generally protected through a mix of usernames and passwords, as well as several levels of restricted access. You can then implement even more security measures to prevent your high-level data from being accessed when it shouldn't. Even with all of these precautions, it is still less than the standard blockchain security protocols that make it perfectly clear who created which blocks and the time and place they created those blocks.

These measures ensure that every transaction is always completed with the full knowledge of the creator, who can then confirm, and sign off on the transaction. This, of course, assumes that the individuals aren't adding information directly to the node. The signature is then further confirmed before the block can be attached to the chain. Even if a username and password combination is not required for users to have access, the chain will still automatically log the IP address of any user who creates new blocks.

Data Alteration

If you think that you are going to need to alter data that is being stored in a blockchain, then blockchain technology might not be right for you and your business. With a centralized database, its simple to alter data by merely tracking down the appropriate clearance, changing the required data, and having those changes saved in a log. With blockchain technology, the only way to do the same with data that has already been stored is to simultaneously change the data across 51 percent of the nodes that are available on the network. While this is a useful security feature of blockchains, in some scenarios, it will automatically disqualify blockchain databases from running in several others.

Data Restoration

If you find yourself doing nothing but updating backup data, then you might discover blockchain technology beneficial. When you use a traditional database, you have to instigate backups manually, leaving you to worry about making sure that everything is where it needs to be. On the other hand, when it comes to a distributed database, the information in it is automatically updated across all available nodes every time new information is added to the chain. As long as all of your nodes don't catastrophically fail at the same time, then you don't have anything to worry about.

Depending on the costs that are associated with backing up and updating all of your data, you may find that the additional operating expenses associated with a decentralized database may make it the cheaper of the two alternatives.

Easy to Share

Centralized databases are often limited concerning access, while a blockchain database can be temporarily connected to another blockchain database easily. This ability to connect to other blockchain databases makes the process of transferring information between the too, nearly painless.

The other blockchains that you are connecting to could be related to a specific department within your company, or even related to entirely different companies. If you are considering doing this, it is essential to keep in mind that when you give someone access to your blockchain, you are giving them access to your entire blockchain. This may require significant planning to effectively utilize if you deal with sensitive information.

Storage Limitations

One area where a traditional database beats a blockchain database is in the amount of data that can be comfortably stored.

When a new node is created in a decentralized database, the entirety of the blockchain is downloaded to it. This, along with the fact that nodes can be thousands and thousands of miles apart from one another, means that it is in your best interest to keep the total amount of data in your blockchain manageable. As a general point of reference, the database for Bitcoin only has about 100 gigabytes, and it has been around for nearly ten years. If you need a high capacity option, you might need to look elsewhere.

Verification Process

If you are planning on running a private blockchain, then you don't need to worry about funding a reward for the validation of blocks. In fact, you won't even have to worry about a proof of work system at all. Instead, you will want to use a proof of stake model, because everyone in the private blockchain will have a stake in keeping the chain up-to-date and reliable. This means that the process for validating blocks can be more straightforward. However, you will still need to factor in the amount of time it will take to process and ensure that you have the workforce to facilitate the work.

Taking the Next Step

After analyzing the specifics, if you decide to take advantage of blockchain technology, it is crucial that you consider exactly how you plan to use the technology.

If you are an existing business owner, who hope to get ahead of the curve, then you'll want to focus your attention and energy on the potential ways that blockchain and smart technology can work together to improve the ancillary aspects of your business. More specifically, you'll want to take a long look at things that have the potential to decrease costs and improve efficiency.

This means that you will need to consider all the many ways that utilizing blockchain will make you more competitive in the eyes of your competition by allowing you to get a jump start on emerging trends in your industry.

Alternately, you will need to consider the various disruptions to the way your business works that implementing blockchain technology might bring to light.

This will require you to move things around now so that the disruptions you might experience are kept to a minimum. Being aware of what is likely to happen next will make it a lot easier to face head-on.

If you are considering forming a new business based around blockchain, then you'll want to work with as many different blockchains as possible. This will help you to improve your grasp of the technology, as well as to help to make the technology more mainstream, which is what is needed for new blockchain companies to take off.

If you hope to break into the mainstream with the help of blockchain, then you will want to do everything you can to ensure blockchain technology becomes mainstream.

You also want to keep in mind that it is, more than likely, going to be a tough road to travel. However, many of the most significant benefits of blockchain technology are only going to be available to companies who have an existing infrastructure already in place to take full advantage of them.

This means that the most realistic forecast for the rise of blockchain technology is that there will be a handful of companies that are going to come along and grab a share of the spotlight, leaving the rest of the room at the top being taken up by the members of the old guard who can get their acts together and make a move on blockchain technology before their competition.

BLOCKCHAIN IMPLEMENTATION MISTAKES TO AVOID

With all the hype that surrounds blockchains, it can be easy to leap into the fray without looking at how to implement your own blockchain distribution system. This is a huge mistake. Before you can take the plunge, you need to make sure that you are avoiding the following errors.

Having Unrealistic Expectations

If you are planning on being able to use a blockchain efficiently, the first thing that you need to understand is that it is not a catchall solution to every problem. Fortunately, you can set up a private system, and only a handful of people will have to know if the initial testing goes poorly.

This also goes for the amount of information that is routinely stored in each block. The bulk of the entire blockchain will ultimately be duplicated to each new node that is created, so an extremely bloated chain will be adding unnecessary bloat to all of the computers using the blockchain. It is essential to keep in mind that the entire Bitcoin blockchain is only 55 gigs. While this is great when it comes to storing private databases securely, it is not the best choice when it comes to the usage of large-scale data. This these cases a centralized data storage system will be the better choice.

It is also important to remember, that while blockchain systems have numerous fail-safes in place to prevent user error, it doesn't mean that they are infallible. Since each block is only referred to by a hash key, it makes it much more likely for humans to mistake blocks for other blocks to everyone's detriment. So, if you are going to utilize blockchains in your business, you need to be sure to implement a failsafe to check for this kind of thing to have the best results.

Underestimating the Time Commitment

It will take a lot of time to understand the intricacies of blockchain technology fully. If you plan on seeing the implementation of a blockchain system through to completion, you have to understand precisely how much time is required to learn to utilize blockchain technology to its fullest potential. After reading this book, you will still need to do more research to understand the best way for you to implement a blockchain that best serves the purposes of your business. This means that you will need to understand what you are going to be using blockchains for on a regular basis, but also what any secondary or tertiary duties might include.

Only after you have a clear idea of what you are going to be using the blockchain system for, you will be able to determine which kind of creation software is going to be right for you and your needs. The market for blockchain creation tools isn't crowded, which means you need to know exactly what you are looking for regarding finding one that is reliable and effective. Making a poor decision on this will make the creation process more difficult than it needs to be.

Being Impatient

After you have a clear understanding of how you are going to use your blockchain distributed database and how you are going to implement the blockchain, it is essential that you not hurry to finish the process. When it comes to implementing blockchain technology you have to take things at a more measured pace. The process can be long and complicated, but you must follow it through to the letter as well as testing it thoroughly before you begin to rely on the blockchain in a real-world setting. Setting up a good blockchain takes time, and rushing will only cause you problems.

Keeping this in mind, it is vital that you decide on a timetable that accurately reflects how long it will take you to complete the project. You need to make sure that you consider the time that it will take to get buy-in from anyone else whose opinion is required before you can start the process.

Not Limiting Access

When it comes to exciting new technologies like blockchain, it's natural for numerous people to be interested in testing it out. If you are running a private blockchain, then it is crucial that you not let too many people have access until they've received proper training. Your fledgling blockchain can become easily derailed if you allow even a few inexperienced hands at the help. When it comes to accessing the core of the blockchain in a private system, you need to be sure to store the key for private access that is generated with a new blockchain in a safe location, because if it is lost, there will be no way for you to regain control of the blockchain.

A Look At Cryptocurrency and Bitcoin's Past

Cryptocurrencies are digital currencies which are electronic in nature. They do not have a physical form like paper money or coins which you probably have in your wallet right now. You can't hold them physically, but you can buy things with them.

Depending on the merchant you're doing business with, they may accept more than one cryptocurrency as payment.

According to CoinMarketCap (https://coinmarketcap.com), there are more than 1,000 active cryptocurrencies right now. If you're looking to invest your hard-earned cash but can't afford Bitcoin prices right now, there are plenty of alternative cryptocurrencies to choose from such as Ethereum, Litecoin, Ripple, Dash, Monero, Zcash, and more.

We would, of course, advise you to do some in-depth research on the cryptocurrency you want to invest in as not all cryptocurrencies are equal. Some are more stable than others and would, therefore, make for better investments.

Bitcoin is not the world's first cryptocurrency, but it is the most successful.

Many have come before it but all have failed. And the reason for failure?

Virtual currency had an inherent problem – it was easy to double spend.

You could pay $100 to one merchant and use the same amount of money to pay a second merchant! Scammers and fraudsters simply loved this loophole.

Fortunately, in 2007, Satoshi Nakamoto started working on the Bitcoin concept. On October 31st the following year, he released his white paper entitled *"Bitcoin: A Peer-to-Peer Electronic Cash System"* which outlined a payment system that addressed the double spending problem of digital currencies.

It was a brilliant concept that drew the attention of the cryptographic community. The Bitcoin Project software was registered in SourceForge just a little over a week after the white paper was published.

In January 2009, the first ever Bitcoin block called the 'Genesis block' was mined. Days later, block 170 recorded the first ever Bitcoin transaction between Hal Finney and Satoshi Nakamoto.

The very next year, in November 2010, Bitcoin's market cap exceeded $1,000,000! This was a very pivotal moment in the development of Bitcoin as this lead to more people getting interested and investing in Bitcoins. The price at this point was $0.50/BTC.

However, in June 2011, Bitcoin experienced the so-called "Great Bubble of 2011" after reaching an all-time high of $31.91/BTC. Just 4 days after reaching its highest price, the exchange rate plummeted to just $10/BTC.

Many investors panicked at losing so much money and sold at a loss. It took almost 2 years for the exchange rate to recover and surpass the previous all-time high. Those who kept their Bitcoins made the right decision as the price has continued to climb and surpass everyone's expectations.

What's really interesting about Bitcoin is that while all transactions are public and nothing is hidden from anyone, no one actually knows anything about Satoshi Nakamoto.

Many have speculated that he is not just one person but rather a collective pseudonym for a group of cryptographic developers. Some have come forward claiming to be Satoshi, but to date, his real identity remains a secret.

Why Do Cryptocurrencies Exist?

Many people have started thinking that cryptocurrencies, Bitcoin in particular, are on the brink of replacing our national currencies such as the US Dollar, British Pound Sterling, Euro, Canadian Dollars, and more. This is because cryptocurrencies have started to become very viable alternatives to traditional currency.

Cryptocurrencies exist to address weaknesses in traditional currencies which are, of course, backed by central banks and governments. This makes traditional currencies prone to corruption and manipulation, among a host of other issues.

Unlike traditional currencies, there is no governing body that backs Bitcoin and other cryptocurrencies which means they aren't subjected to anybody's whims.

Bitcoin is completely decentralized, open source and transparent. This means that you can see all the transactions that have ever been done on the network and you can check and review the blockchain data yourself to verify the authenticity of each transaction.

Bitcoin runs on highly complex mathematical algorithms to regulate the creation of new Bitcoins and to make sure no double spending ever occurs

on the network (remember, this is the Achilles' heel of failed virtual currencies before Bitcoin).

The Bitcoin code is so secure and advanced that it's virtually impossible to cheat the system so if you're thinking you can create an unlimited number of Bitcoins, you're greatly mistaken.

One of the main problems of traditional currency is that these aren't limited in number. This means that governments and central banks can print more money when they see fit.

When more money is printed and enters the economy, this reduces the purchasing power of our paper money which means we need to spend

more for an item we've only spent a few dollars on before; this is called inflation.

Bitcoin, on the other hand, is a different story. The Bitcoin Protocol states that only 21,000,000 Bitcoins can ever be mined and created which means that Bitcoin is, in fact, a scarce resource.

Also, like national currencies, Bitcoins are divisible, much like cents to a dollar. The smallest Bitcoin unit is called a Satoshi, and it is 1/100,000,000 of a Bitcoin. This means you can invest a few thousand Satoshis at a time until you finally get a whole Bitcoin.

Of course, if you go this route, it may take you some time to get to 1 BTC but if the price continues to skyrocket, then buying a few Satoshis regularly may pay off in the long term.

Another reason why cryptocurrencies are gaining in popularity is that it is highly portable which means you can bring it with you anywhere you go. You can do the same with physical money and gold. However, a large amount will lead to a heavy load on your wallet or bag.

Try putting a million dollars in a briefcase or carrying a bag of gold! It's certainly not as light as it looks in movies.

With cryptocurrency, you have different wallet choices, all of which are highly portable, so you can easily make payments whenever and wherever you want.

Bitcoins are not subject to bank and government regulations. This means you don't need to pay those hefty bank fees which you incur whenever you send payments to other people.

You also don't need to wait several hours or maybe even a few days for your payments to clear or post as Bitcoin payments are made almost instantly (usually in 10-45 minutes).

How Bitcoin Works

In this section, we will do our best to explain the Bitcoin process as simply as possible without going into too much technical jargon.

The first thing you need to do is get yourself some Bitcoins. You can either mine this yourself, receive some as payment for goods or services, or buy at a Bitcoin exchange like Coinbase or Kraken. There are different wallets for you to store your new Bitcoins in.

You can use a desktop wallet, mobile app wallet, paper wallet, hardware wallet or an online wallet. There are pros and cons to each type of wallet.

However, most experts agree that online wallets, specifically those on exchange sites, are not so secure because both your private and public keys are saved online. This makes your wallet highly vulnerable to hackers.

When you've selected the most suitable wallet for your needs, you can then start making Bitcoin transactions. To send Bitcoin to another user, all you have to do is just get their email or Bitcoin address, enter the amount you wish to send, write a quick note to tell them what the payment is for (this is optional), and hit the Send button!

Alternatively, if you've got the QR code to their Bitcoin wallet, you can simply scan it and hit Send. The transaction will appear in the other person's account in a short period of time, usually between 10-45 minutes.

The reason for this 'wait' is explained more fully in the next section.

And that's it! Bitcoin transactions are quick, safe, cheap and the perfect alternative to paying with bank-issued credit and debit cards, and even paying in cash.

The Technology Behind Bitcoin

On the surface, Bitcoin transactions appear to be fast and easy – and they truly are. However, behind the scenes, the technology that makes the Bitcoin network run seamlessly is a massive ledger known as the blockchain.

It's massive because it contains a record of all Bitcoin transactions that have ever taken place since Bitcoin was first released in 2009.

As more time passes by and more transactions occur, the size of the blockchain will continue to grow. So here is how the blockchain works:

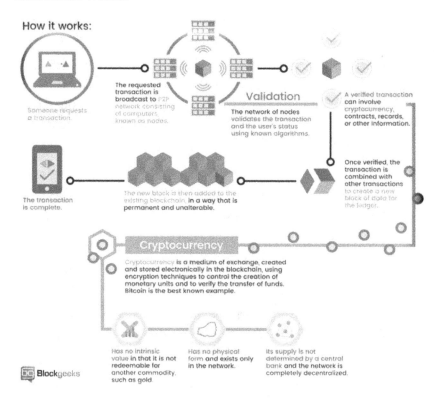

(Image Source: BlockGeeks.com)

When you send a payment, your wallet or app sends out a request to the entire Bitcoin network which is made up of computers or nodes. These nodes then validate your transaction using known algorithms.

Once your transaction is verified and confirmed, it is then combined with other transactions to create a new block of data for the blockchain.

This new block is then added to the end of the blockchain. When this happens, the transaction becomes complete and is now permanent.

This entire process takes about 10-45 minutes from start to finish (this is why Bitcoin transactions don't happen instantly). Once the transaction is finalized, no one can undo or delete the transaction. The person you've sent the Bitcoin payment to (the receiver) will now see your payment in his wallet.

So who verifies and confirms transactions if there's no central body governing the network?

The answer is the miners. The miners are literally the lifeblood of the entire Bitcoin network. Some have even compared miners to being hamsters in the wheel that keep the entire Bitcoin network going! And this is true.

Miners play such a huge role in the success of Bitcoin that they truly deserve getting rewarded in precious Bitcoins. Without them, no new blocks would be created and added to the blockchain.

If nothing is added to the blockchain, no transactions are ever finalized. This means no Bitcoins payments are sent and received by anyone on the network. No new Bitcoins will be created.

Because miners are indispensable to the Bitcoin network, they are compensated for their hard work in terms of Bitcoins (it would not make any sense to reward them in traditional paper currency). They are almost like employees of the network.

Since there are only a limited number of Bitcoins (21 million), the number of Bitcoins that miners are paid with will continue to dwindle until all Bitcoins are exhausted by around 2140.

Now that you know what Bitcoin and cryptocurrency are all about, let's go to the next guide where you will learn how the value of Bitcoin is determined.

Bitcoin Value – How Is The Value Of Bitcoin Determined

Bitcoin has been getting a huge amount of hype recently. It's one of the many digital currencies in existence today which acts and functions like regular money but exists entirely electronically—like data inside computers.

And that can be kind of confusing, because if there is no actual physical Bitcoin:

How can it have value?

How can you use digital currency in a physical world?

Well actually, the question of how Bitcoin has any value at all isn't so far off from the question of how most real-world money has value.

First off, Bitcoin has no actual intrinsic value, which means that it has little to no use to us outside of its economic context. But the same can be said for most real-world currencies: money only has value because the government that issues it says it does.

This is called 'fiat currency,' because its value is not tied to any physical commodity and relies on the backing of a government.

But unlike fiat currency, Bitcoin does not have an issuing authority that gives it value. Bitcoin is a decentralized currency, meaning there is no governing body that regulates its production and transactions.

It doesn't answer to any government or organization, so there isn't really a reason why it should have value, yet it does - and it can all be boiled down to utility, scarcity, and supply and demand.

Bitcoin's Value Lies In Its Utility

Before we discuss the utility of Bitcoin, first you must understand the basics of how it works. You are connected to the community of Bitcoin users through a computer network, and the ledgers that Bitcoin uses is called a blockchain: transactions are compiled into blocks, which in turn are connected in a chain-like manner, hence the name.

The ledger keepers are called miners, because what they are doing, essentially, sounds very much like gold miners who work hard to find gold: they are working for the reward in the form of Bitcoins, which, like gold, are limited in supply.

So now you know how Bitcoin works. What does that have to do with its

value? Everything, actually. Bitcoin's value is in its utility: its decentralization, security, and ease of transaction.

First, let's look at Bitcoin's decentralized system. Bitcoin is designed such that there is no need for any governing authority to control it. It operates through a peer-to-peer network where all transactions are recorded in the blockchain.

On the most basic level, this would mean that it is not tied to any state and therefore is the only truly borderless currency. What this means is that you can conduct transactions with people from different countries easily because you're using the same currency.

On a deeper, much more complicated level, the decentralization of Bitcoin's system creates the possibility of transforming the finance industry.

The finance industry offers multiple ways to simplify transactions for ease of convenience. There are credit and debit cards, money transferring systems, electronic bank transfers, etc. But all of these systems need to have a middleman to function—they need a company or authority to facilitate the exchange.

And what you're doing whenever you make a transaction is that you're putting your trust on the middleman—that they will get your money through or keep your money safe among other things. There is also the matter of transaction fees, which, considered per transaction, is not too much, but can easily pile up over time. What Bitcoin does is it eliminates the need for these middlemen.

As mentioned above, all transactions in the Bitcoin network are recorded in the blockchain by miners. While the blockchain and miner network has the semblance of a governing body in the sense that it keeps track of all Bitcoins in existence, it's still in the public domain and therefore cannot be monopolized.

This means that no single person or group of persons has a hold on the network—which, in turn, means that Bitcoins can remain fully transparent and neutral in its transactions.

But if there is no official body acting as a regulator, who can you trust to make sure that transactions do go through? The answer: no one. And it sounds bad, but it's actually a good thing.

The Bitcoin system is designed to operate without the need for trust. See, it's not simply a digital currency, it's a *crypto*currency, which means that it is heavily based on encryption techniques to keep it safe.

Instead of operating based on customer trust, Bitcoin operates using tried and tested mathematics (more on that later). Cheating the network is impossible due to its public environment.

Not only that, but the system is encrypted so that trying to commit fraud would require an *extremely large* amount of computing power, which would by then have been more useful if you just used it to mine more Bitcoins.

The security system, aside from ensuring the reliability of Bitcoin transactions, also ensures that the identity of the Bitcoin users can be protected. Unlike in credit cards, your account number does not have any value in your transactions, which are ultimately verified using a private and public key.

It works like this: you put a digital signature to your transactions using your private key which can be verified by the users of the network using your public key. The keys are encrypted so that the public key can only ever work if you had used the correct private key in the first place.

This means that:

Your identity can't be stolen by criminals to make fraudulent transactions in your name.

You can choose to remain completely anonymous in the Bitcoin network, which may prove useful for some.

Lastly, Bitcoins have the possibility of providing an ease of convenience that surpasses the traditional paying methods that we already have now.

According to the Bitcoin site, using Bitcoins allow you "to send and receive Bitcoins anywhere in the world at any time.

No bank holidays. No borders. No bureaucracy. Bitcoin allows its users to be in full control of their money."

Bitcoins Are Incredibly Scarce

Fiat currency has a technically unlimited supply in the sense that governments can produce money whenever they want. Obviously, they don't do that because it will lead to inflation, so the production and release of money is controlled by the government based on intensive research on market trends and needs. Bitcoin, as you might have guessed, does not work the same.

Because Bitcoin is decentralized, there is no authority that decides when to make new Bitcoins. The system is designed so that new Bitcoins can only be created as part of a reward system for the miners.

And the reward is well-deserved: the backbone of the Bitcoin system is cryptography, or the art of writing and solving codes which requires a hefty amount of work to solve.

To update the blockchain, miners from all over the world have to race to solve a specific math problem called SHA-256, which stands for Secure Hash Algorithm 256 bit.

It's basically a math problem wherein you're given an output and you're supposed to find the input, like solving for x and y given that $x + y = 2$.

The only way to solve this kind of problem is through guesswork, and to solve the SHA-256, you'd have to go through an *insane* amount of possible solutions before you find the answer—for which you'd need an extremely powerful (not to mention expensive) computer.

Miners invest a lot of money on these supercomputers (as well as the huge amount of electricity it needs to run) all to mine new Bitcoins.

Jason Bloomberg, in an article for Forbes, writes that the value of Bitcoin is representative of this effort: because mining Bitcoins take hard work, they become more valuable.So, first point to its scarcity is that Bitcoins are hard to come by. You'd need a sizeable investment just to be able to create new Bitcoins.

But they're even made scarcer due to the fact that there can only ever be a certain number of Bitcoins in existence, which is 21 million. (If you're wondering why 21 million, it's basically because that's what's written in the source code.)

The cap on Bitcoin production is there to ensure that Bitcoin wouldn't ever be hyperinflated.

It's even designed to be produced steadily: the reward system goes by half every 210,000 blocks added to the chain (i.e., every four years), with the SHA-256 problems even varying in difficulty depending on the amount of miners—more miners mean harder problems to ensure that not too many Bitcoins get produced all at once.

Projecting from this trend, the last Bitcoin is estimated to be mined around the year 2140. To put things in perspective, there are about 16.74 million Bitcoins in existence at the time of writing.

That fewer and fewer Bitcoins can be mined as time goes by drives up the interest of the people in the currency, because rarity is desirable and highly marketable.

This increases the value of Bitcoin, because it operates using a network— the larger the network, the greater use you can get out of Bitcoin.

Supply and Demand Affects Bitcoin Value Directly

The market value of Bitcoin—that is, the money that people are willing to pay for it—follows the same old basic demand and supply rule: a high demand increases its price and a low demand decreases it.

Before we go in any further, just remember that the value of something is not the same as its price; value is what people perceive a product is worth, while price is what they pay for it. Even so, value and price go hand in hand: the price of something is directly related to its value and vice versa.

According to an article in the Economist, the increasing trend in the price of Bitcoin is what drives people to invest in it.

People are investing because they believe that, following the trend so far, they would be able to sell their Bitcoins for a much higher price in the future—which the article argues is a perfect example of the greater-fool theory.

Basically, the greater-fool theory states that the price of a product is determined not by its intrinsic value, but by the beliefs and expectations that the consumers put on the product.

From this perspective, the surging price of Bitcoin serves not to increase its actual value, but to render it irrelevant.

The market is driving the price of Bitcoin up because of growing belief that it will be worth more in the future, not because they think its value is increasing over time. However, some people argue that the surge in Bitcoin prices that the past year has seen is not indicative of it being a bubble.

In the Bitcoin site itself, it argues that it is not a bubble, citing that bubbles are artificially overvaluations of a product which tends to correct itself eventually.

It cites its relatively small and young market as the reason for the volatility in Bitcoin prices—that "choices based on individual human action by hundreds of thousands of market participants is the cause for Bitcoin's price to fluctuate as the market seeks price discovery."

It argues that the volatility of Bitcoin prices are due to many forces such as:

Loss of confidence in Bitcoin

A large difference between value and price not based on the fundamentals of the Bitcoin economy

Increased press coverage stimulating speculative demand

Fear of uncertainty

And old-fashioned irrational exuberance and greed

As such, Bitcoin is arguing that its growing prices can be attributed to more and more people finding the product increasingly worth their money based on its utility, thereby validating its value.

So, in summary: Bitcoin's utility and scarcity gives it value, but its prices seem to send opposing signals as to whether it's truly valuable or not.

With more and more people beginning to show interest in Bitcoin, perhaps we are barely scratching the surface of what its true value may be.

Mine Your Own Bitcoin

Bitcoin miners play an extremely important role in the Bitcoin network. Without miners, there would be no new Bitcoins, and no transactions would be confirmed. Bitcoin miners are so important to the Bitcoin ecosystem that they are justly rewarded with Bitcoins for their hard work. However, Bitcoin mining is not as profitable as it seems.

When Bitcoin was still in its infancy, miners were getting paid 50 Bitcoins for every block mined. But every 210,000 blocks (this is around 4 years), the reward is halved. So this means that the initial 50 Bitcoins was halved into 25 Bitcoins.

And now, at this particular point in time, the block reward is down to 12.5 Bitcoins. If you consider the price for one Bitcoin right now (well over $10,000), this is still is a very attractive reward indeed. And experts predict the price will continue to go up as the number of Bitcoins in existence slowly go up, too, and the demand for more Bitcoins continue to increase.

Mining Bitcoins is not an easy job, much like any other physical mining job in the real world. Bitcoin miners may not get dirty from soot and mud, but their powerful computers do.

The difficulty in mining new blocks has gone up so much that individual miners are finding it extremely difficult to solve complex cryptographic functions on their own. Many different miners or mining groups compete to discover a new block and the mining difficulty are at extremely high levels now.

Most, if not all, miners are forced to work in mining pools where several miners work together as a group to add new transactions to the blockchain. When a new block is mined, the reward is split according to the work each miner's computer has done.

Mining Bitcoins doesn't come cheap. You can't just use any computer as solving cryptographic functions will take so much of your computer's processing power.

Not even a high-end laptop or desktop computer can do the job anymore – it's really that difficult to mine new Bitcoin blocks today!

Even if you join mining pools, you'll need to invest a lot of money to buy the right hardware. In the beginning, a powerful CPU (Computer Processing Unit) and GPU (Graphical Processing Unit) were sufficient to mine new blocks. However, as the difficulty of mining Bitcoins have gone up, more processing power was needed.

Today, an ASIC (Application Specific Integrated Circuit) chip is seen as the only way to succeed in mining. A Bitcoin-mining ASIC chip is designed specifically to mine Bitcoins. It can't do any other task apart from mining Bitcoins.

While this may be viewed as a downside for some, remember that mining is a hard job. You need all the resources you can use to find the next transaction block so you can add it to the blockchain and get rewarded Bitcoins in the process. Professional miners find this hardware very powerful than other technologies used in the past.

Also, it's not as power hungry as other hardware out there. It will still consume plenty of power, however, so consider that if you're worried about your electricity bills.

If you are prepared to buy the technology to mine Bitcoins as well as pay more costly power bills, then mining Bitcoins will be a great way for you to acquire this particular cryptocurrency.

However, we'd like to say that this is not a job for the uninitiated. It's best to leave this task to the experts or those with an in-depth knowledge of how Bitcoin mining works. As we've shown you in this guide, there are many ways you can acquire Bitcoins that don't require a healthy investment of both time and money.

In the next chapter, we'll go into more detail on Bitcoin mining, and you'll see for yourself if this is something you want to get involved in.

Bitcoin Mining – Everything You Need to Know About Bitcoin Mining

In this guide, we'll cover everything there is to know about Bitcoin mining so you can find out if this is something that you would like to do so you can get your fair share of Bitcoins.

Bitcoin has been in the news a lot nowadays, and its current price is a source of interest to a lot of people around the world. A few years ago, many people labeled Bitcoin as a scam, but now it is seen, along with other cryptocurrencies, as the future of money.

Cryptocurrencies, as virtual or digital currencies, have no physical properties and need to be 'mined' electronically.

Before we go into details, we'd like to define first the most common terms used in Bitcoin mining so you can easily understand how this highly technical process works.

Bitcoin Mining Terms You Should Get to Know

Block: The data related to transactions is stored on a page known as a block.

Bitcoins Per Block: This is the number of Bitcoins rewarded to miners for every block mined and added to the blockchain. The initial reward per block was 50 Bitcoins but every 210,000 blocks, the reward is divided by 2. Currently, the reward sits at 12.5 Bitcoins per block.

Bitcoin Difficulty: With an increasing number of miners, Bitcoin mining also increases in difficulty. The ideal average mining time defined by the network is 10 minutes per block.

Electricity Rate: To calculate how much you're earning, you need to check your electric bill. This can help you judge how much electricity is consumed by your mining computer in return for your Bitcoin earnings. Are you making a profit, breaking even or losing? These are important questions all miners need to ask themselves.

Hash: In Bitcoin mining, a hash can be seen as a problem related to mathematics. The mining machine needs to solve it to earn rewards.

Hash Rate: The time it takes to solve these hash problems is called Hash Rate. Hash rate increases with the number of miners on the Bitcoin network. MH/s (Mega hash per second), GH/s (Giga hash per second), TH/s (Terra hash per second) and PH/s (Peta hash per second) are some of the units that are used in measuring hash rates.

Pool Fees: Miners join a pool for mining known as a 'mining pool.' Like natural mining, miners here mine together as it helps them solve those complex hash problems faster. You have to pay fees to the pool so it can continue its operations. When Bitcoins are finally mined, they are distributed to miners with respect to their hash rates.

Power Consumption: Not every mining machine consumes the same amount of electricity. So before buying yourself an expensive machine, you must check first how much power it will consume.

Time Frame: This is a duration that you need to define yourself to see how much you're mining. For example, you define a time frame of 45 days. This means that after 45 days, you'll calculate how many Bitcoins you've mined during this period. Defining a time frame can help you see if you are producing more or less than your fellow miners.

Bitcoin Mining Hardware Commonly Used by Miners

CPU (Computer Processing Unit):

In the beginning, Bitcoin mining was incredibly easy and could be easily mined on regular desktop CPUs. However, as the number of miners increased, Bitcoin mining on CPU became more difficult and caused computer hard drives to fail.

GPU (Graphical Processing Unit):

With a surge in the number of miners on the network, the use of GPUs started to gain popularity when people realized they were more efficient for Bitcoin mining.

Some advanced GPUs even allowed miners to increase their mining productivity 50-100 times better in comparison to CPU mining. People also started altering their BIOS settings to maximize their rewards. Nvidia and ATI's cards shot to popularity as a result.

FPGA (Field-Programmable Gate Array):

FPGA is an integrated circuit created with the objective of performing Bitcoin mining. GPU mining was turning out to be not so profitable for everyone because of rising electricity costs. FPGA was designed to consume less power, and so miners moved from GPUs to FPGAs.

ASIC (Application-Specific Integrated Circuit):

With the arrival of ASIC technology, FPGA was overtaken as the primary hardware used in Bitcoin mining. ASIC is a computer chip that is used solely for mining of cryptocurrencies like Bitcoins or other coins that use the SHA-256 algorithm.

Unlike other mining hardware, ASICs cannot be used to do tasks other than mining. Right now, this is the gold standard which miners swear by as these powerful chips solve more problems in less time while consuming less electricity as well.

The Role of Mining In The Creation Of New Bitcoins

You can own Bitcoins using a few methods. The easiest way is to buy some Bitcoins on a Bitcoin exchange platform though, of course, Bitcoin prices are so high now that you'll need to make a sizeable investment.

The other method is not to use any money and instead simply mine Bitcoins using computer hardware.

It's important to note here that the main and integral purpose of mining is the creation or release of new Bitcoins which can be then available on the network.

Currently, about 16 million Bitcoins have already been mined out of the possible 21 million Bitcoins that can ever be created.

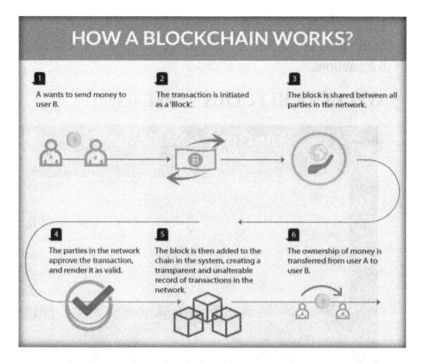

HOW A BLOCKCHAIN WORKS?

1 A wants to send money to user B.

2 The transaction is initiated as a 'Block'.

3 The block is shared between all parties in the network.

4 The parties in the network approve the transaction, and render it as valid.

5 The block is then added to the chain in the system, creating a transparent and unalterable record of transactions in the network.

6 The ownership of money is transferred from user A to user B.

(Image Source: Biz2Credit)

Unlike normal currency transactions being confirmed and regulated through banks, cryptocurrencies' transactional data appears a public ledger known as the 'blockchain'.

Each block can be said as a page that contains the data of transactions. That is why it is called as blockchain. Mining helps to confirm these transactions on a blockchain.

Miners also run cryptographic hash on blocks. A hash requires complex computations.

These hashes are important because they make a block secure. Once a block has been accepted in the blockchain then it can't be altered. Miners anonymously validate these transactions.

For their help, miners are rewarded Bitcoins. 'Proof of work' is the term coined for the assistance of miners in validating transactions.

WHAT IS BITCOIN MINING?

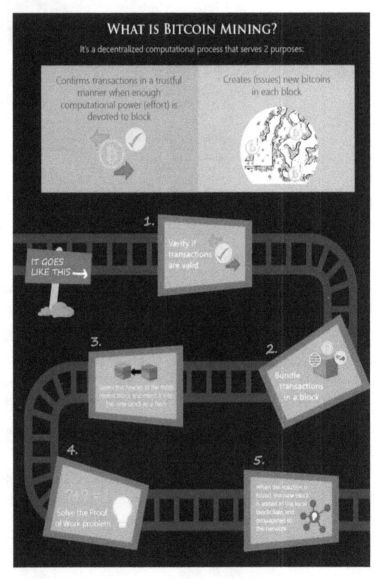

(Image Source: BitcoinMining.com)

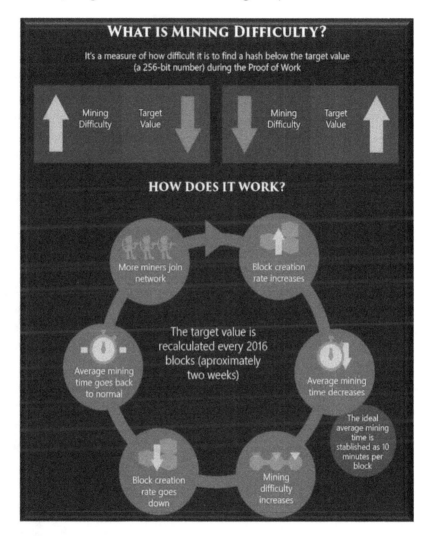

(Image Source: BitcoinMining.com)

Is Bitcoin Mining Profitable?

Bitcoin mining is the process of earning bitcoin in exchange for running the verification process to validate bitcoin transactions. These transactions provide security for the Bitcoin network which in turn compensates miners by giving them bitcoins. Miners can profit if the price of bitcoins exceeds the cost to mine. With recent changes in technology and the creation of professional mining centers with enormous computing power, as well as the shifting price of bitcoin itself, many individual miners are asking themselves, is bitcoin mining still profitable?

There are several factors that determine whether bitcoin mining is a profitable venture. These include the cost of the electricity to power the computer system (cost of electricity), the availability and price of the computer system, and the difficulty in providing the services. Difficulty is measured in the hashes per second of the Bitcoin validation transaction. The hash rate measures the rate of solving the problem—the difficulty changes as more miners enter because the network is designed to produce a certain level of bitcoins every ten minutes. When more miners enter the market, the difficulty increases to ensure that the level is static. The last factor for determining profitability is the price of bitcoins as compared against standard, hard currency.

Source:
https://www.investopedia.com/articles/forex/051115/bitcoin-mining-still-profitable.asp

94

Key Takeaways

1. Bitcoin is mined using computing rigs which include expensive hardware.
2. Miners are rewarded with bitcoin for verifying blocks of transactions to the blockchain network.
3. As more miners compete for bitcoin rewards, the process becomes more difficult.

To determine whether bitcoin mining is profitable for you, consider costs of equipment and electricity as well as the difficulty associated with mining and how the price of bitcoin will impact potential rewards.

Source:
https://www.investopedia.com/articles/forex/051115/bitcoin -mining-still-profitable.asp

The Components of Bitcoin Mining

Prior to the advent of new bitcoin mining software in 2013, mining was generally done on personal computers. But the introduction of application specific integrated circuit chips (ASIC) offered up to 100 billion times the capability of older personal machines, rendering the use of personal computing to mine bitcoins inefficient and obsolete. While bitcoin mining is still theoretically possible with older hardware, there is little question that it is not a profitable venture. This is because of the way that mining is set up: miners are competing to solve hash problems as quickly as possible, so those miners at a serious computational disadvantage essentially stand no chance of solving a problem first and being rewarded with bitcoin. When miners used the old machines, the difficulty in mining bitcoins was roughly in line with the price of bitcoins. But with these new machines came issues related to both the high cost to obtain and run the new equipment and the lack of availability.

Source:
https://www.investopedia.com/articles/forex/051115/bitcoin -mining-still-profitable.asp

Profitability Before and After ASIC

Old timers (say, way back in 2009) mining bitcoins using just their personal computers were able to make a profit for several reasons. First, these miners already owned their systems, so equipment costs were effectively nil. They could change the settings on their computers to run more efficiently with less stress. Second, these were the days before professional bitcoin mining centers with massive computing power entered the game. Early miners only had to compete with other individual miners on home computer systems. The competition was on even footing. Even when electricity costs varied based on geographic region, the difference was not enough to deter individuals from mining.

After ASICs came into play, the game changed. Individuals were now competing against powerful mining rigs that had more computing power. Mining profits were getting chipped away by expenses like purchasing new computing equipment, paying higher energy costs for running the new equipment, and the continued difficulty in mining.

Source:
https://www.investopedia.com/articles/forex/051115/bitcoin -mining-still-profitable.asp

Difficulty of Mining Bitcoin

As discussed above, the difficulty rate associated with mining bitcoin is variable and changes roughly every two weeks in order to maintain a stable production of verified blocks for the blockchain (and, in turn, bitcoins introduced into circulation). The higher the difficulty rate, the less likely that an individual miner is to successfully be able to solve the hash problem and earn bitcoin. In recent years, the mining difficulty rate has skyrocketed. When bitcoin was first launched, the difficulty was 1. As of May 2020, it is more than 16 trillion. This provides an idea of just how many times more difficult it is to mine for bitcoin now than it was a decade ago.

Source:
https://www.investopedia.com/articles/forex/051115/bitcoin-mining-still-profitable.asp

Shifting Rewards

The Bitcoin network will be capped at 21 million total bitcoin. This has been a key stipulation of the entire ecosystem since it was founded, and the limit is put in place to attempt to control for supply of the cryptocurrency. Currently, over 18 million bitcoin have been mined. As a way of controlling the introduction of new bitcoin into circulation, the network protocol halves the number of bitcoin rewarded to miners for successfully completing a block about every four years. Initially, the number of bitcoin a miner received was 50. In 2012, this number was halved and the reward became 25. In 2016, it halved again to 12.5. In May 2020, the reward halved once again to 6.25, the current reward. Prospective miners should be aware that the reward size will decrease into the future, even as difficulty is liable to increase.

Source:
https://www.investopedia.com/articles/forex/051115/bitcoin -mining-still-profitable.asp

Profitability in Today's Environment

Bitcoin mining can still make sense and be profitable for some individuals. Equipment is more easily obtained, although competitive ASICs cost anywhere from a few hundred dollars up to about $10,000. In an effort to stay competitive, some machines have adapted. For example, some hardware allows users to alter settings to lower energy requirements, thus lowering overall costs. Prospective miners should perform a cost/benefit analysis to understand their breakeven price before making the fixed-cost purchases of the equipment.

The variables needed to make this calculation are:

1. Cost of power: what is your electricity rate? Keep in mind that rates change depending on the season, the time of day, and other factors. You can find this information on your electric bill measured in kWh.
2. Efficiency: how much power does your system consume, measured in watts?
3. Time: what is the anticipated length of time you will spend mining?
4. Bitcoin value: what is the value of a bitcoin in U.S. dollars or other official currency?

There are several web-based profitability calculators, such as the one provided by CryptoCompare, that would-be miners can use to analyze the cost/benefit equation of bitcoin mining. Profitability calculators differ slightly and some are more complex than others.

Run your analysis several times using different price levels for both the cost of power and value of bitcoins. Also, change the level of difficulty to see how that impacts the analysis. Determine at what price level bitcoin mining becomes profitable for you—that is your breakeven price. As of May 2020, the price of bitcoin is hovering around $8,000. Given a current reward of 6.25 BTC for a completed block, miners are rewarded around $50,000 for successfully completing a hash. Of course, as the price of bitcoin is highly variable, this reward figure is likely to change.

To compete against the mining mega centers, individuals can join a mining pool, which is a group of miners who work together and share the rewards. This can increase the speed and reduce the difficulty in mining, putting profitability in reach. As difficulty and cost have increased, more and more individual miners have opted to participate in a pool. While the overall reward decreases because it is shared among multiple participants, the combined computing power means that mining pools stand a much greater chance of actually completing a hashing problem first and receiving a reward in the first place.

To answer the question of whether bitcoin mining is still profitable, use a web-based profitability calculator to run a cost-benefit analysis. You can plug in different numbers and find your breakeven point (after which mining is profitable). Determine if you are willing to lay out the necessary initial capital for the hardware, and estimate the future value of bitcoins as well as the level of difficulty. When both bitcoin prices and mining difficulty decline, it usually indicates fewer miners and more ease in receiving bitcoins. When bitcoin prices and mining difficulty rise, expect the opposite—more miners competing for fewer bitcoins.

Source:
https://www.investopedia.com/articles/forex/051115/bitcoin -mining-still-profitable.asp

Online Wallets

Online wallets are most often provided by exchanges, though they're sometimes offered by third parties. Connected to the Internet, they're generally easiest to set up and use. Most only require an email address and a password to create an account, and web wallets are usually designed to provide a simple and straightforward user experience.

Source: *https://www.finder.com/cryptocurrency/wallets*

Mobile Wallets

Mobile wallets are fairly similar to desktop wallets, but they run as an app on your smartphone. Mobile wallets feature many of the same advantages and disadvantages as desktop wallets, with your private key stored on your device. Smartphone wallets are often easier to use than desktop wallets.

Source: *https://www.finder.com/cryptocurrency/wallets*

Desktop Wallet

For starters, desktop wallets are considered to be among the safer options of crypto storage as far as hot wallets go. If you're not aware, hot wallets are those cryptocurrency wallets that are constantly connected to the internet. These include mobile apps, browser-based wallets, exchanges, and so on.

Paper Wallet

To keep it very simple, paper wallets are an offline cold storage method of saving cryptocurrency. It includes printing out your public and private keys on a piece of paper which you then store and save in a secure place. The keys are printed in the form of QR codes which you can scan in the future for all your transactions.

Source: *https://blockgeeks.com/guides/paper-wallet-guide/*

Hardware Wallet

There's a consensus in the Bitcoin community that hardware wallets are the safest Bitcoin wallets and something every serious Bitcoin investor and enthusiast should consider buying. Unlike the other wallet types we've covered so far in this guide, hardware wallets are relatively expensive.

Of course, if you've got a considerable number of Bitcoins to protect, then it's really a small price to pay for keeping your fortune safe. Most hardware wallets support a host of cryptocurrencies so if you've invested in nonBitcoin currencies too, then you'll find this type of wallet to be an excellent purchase.

Hardware wallets are basically powerful and durable USB sticks which you plug into your computer when making a Bitcoin or cryptocurrency transaction. When you're done, simply remove the wallet and store it somewhere safe.

A unique security feature on hardware wallets is the ability to generate private keys offline which means that it's less vulnerable to hacker attacks. These sturdy little devices allow you to bring your private keys anywhere with you without fear of having it exposed to the outside world.

Setup is also quick and easy with hardware wallets. Depending on the wallet, you can assign a PIN code, password, or recovery seed words which you can use to authenticate your access as well as recover your Bitcoins in case your wallet is lost or destroyed.

Just in case you get some form of amnesia and forget your recovery details, you should write down your secret details and hide it somewhere only you know. Otherwise, if someone finds it, either by accident or by design, then your Bitcoins and whatever cryptocurrency you have on there will soon be gone.

Hardware wallets are excellent for storing all your cryptocurrencies safely.

Whether you've got a sizeable collection of digital currency or not, you never have to worry if your wallet will be hacked and your money stolen.

Your private keys are relatively safe. You just need to make sure your memory never fails you, and you'll always remember where you've hidden your wallet backups!

To sum up this guide, the best wallet for your Bitcoins and cryptocurrencies are actually a combination of different wallets. Use hard wallets or paper wallets for long-term storage, desktop wallets for medium-term storage, and web and mobile wallets for short-term storage and frequent transactions.

TRADING OR SELLING CRYPTOCURRENCY FOR PROFIT

Trading and selling your Bitcoin can be a very profitable activity. You probably know someone or heard about someone who bought Bitcoins in the early days when they were worth almost nothing, and ended up selling each Bitcoin for thousands of dollars!

Or you may know people who engage in trading Bitcoins and are profiting very nicely as well. It might seem easy, but the truth is, trading Bitcoins is not for everyone.

Beginners are especially advised to take caution and to be mentally and financially ready before taking the plunge into this exciting high-risk and high-reward world. When trading, it's common sense to follow the 'buy low and sell high' strategy so you can make a profit.

You don't want to sell at a price lower than when you bought in because you'll be selling at a loss. But all these sounds easy on paper.

In the real world, when you're dealing with Bitcoins that's worth hundreds, thousands or even millions of dollars, if you don't have the right mindset and the financial discipline, you could panic very easily.

Especially if you're trading Bitcoins that represent your entire life savings, your retirement fund, or your kids' college tuition!

BITCOIN TRADING STRATEGIES

Common sense and self-control should take precedence over trying to profit thousands of dollars immediately. Here are some Bitcoin trading strategies to guide you on the exchanges.

Practice First

Learning the ins and outs of Bitcoin trading is great, but knowing just theory is different from real-world application. Some Bitcoin exchanges offer a demo account where you can play around and experience real-world trading using real-time prices.

You'll get a feel for the landscape, so to speak, and you'll see for yourself whether you've got the stomach for the high-risk game of Bitcoin trading.

Plan Your Strategy

Investing small amounts at first is a advisable strategy because of the volatility of the cryptocurrency markets.

Popular Bitcoin Trading Platforms

These popular trading platforms will fund your account with a linked bank account or credit card. Normally it takes a few days to weeks to verify your identity through a process call Know Your Customer (KYC). For more trading platforms refer to Top 10 Spot Market Exchanges.

Coinbase Pro

The platform is easy to use, and you can buy, trade, and sell your digital currency.

https://pro.coinbase.com/

Robinhood

The platform is easy to use, and you can buy, trade, and sell your digital currency.

https://robinhood.com

Gemini

The platform is easy to use, and you can buy, trade, and sell your digital currency.

https://exchange.gemini.com/register

Are You Ready To Start Trading Bitcoins?

There are many more Bitcoin and cryptocurrency exchanges we've not been able to include in this guide. It's best to perform due diligence and research before selecting a trading platform. Just remember that whichever cryptocurrency exchange platform you choose to do business with, you must always move your cryptocurrency to a more secure wallet such as a hardware wallet or paper wallet.

Don't leave it in your exchange's wallet as it's at great risk of being stolen by hackers. If you must store some in your online wallet, just keep the smallest amount you can afford to lose.

Using Bitcoin As An Investment Strategy

Bitcoin is a relatively new form of currency which is just starting to gain traction and worldwide acceptance. With the recent exponential growth in the value of Bitcoin, many people are investing in this digital currency to hopefully reap huge profits in the future.

In this guide, we will cover the basics of using Bitcoin as an investment strategy. Note that we are referring to long-term investment here which is not the same as trading Bitcoin for short-term profits.

Investing in the highly volatile cryptocurrency market may not seem like such a good idea for some people. Ideally, you'd have nerves of steel, the discipline and focus to ignore short-term gains, as well as the patience to hold your investment until the right time comes.

If you're really determined to own a small share of the crypto-market, then you should at least know the most suitable methods so you can make the most of your investment.

BITCOIN INVESTMENT METHODS

Dollar Cost Averaging Method

To build long-term wealth, we use a concept called **steady-drip investing**.

Each month, we tuck away a little bit of money, and invest it into a blend of traditional and digital investments (the stock market and the block market).

The Blockchain Investing Flowchart

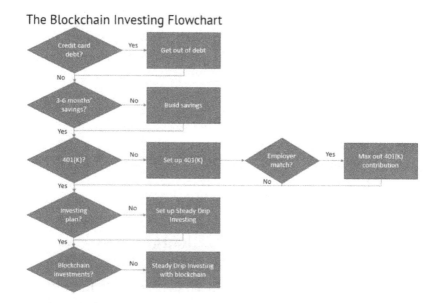

Also called **dollar cost averaging**, the advantage to this method of investing is that you can *set it and forget it.* Every month, like clockwork, it's an auto-withdrawal from your bank account, where your money will go to work for you, building wealth.

Steady-drip investing comes with another advantage: it protects you from yourself. In the world of investing (especially blockchain investing), it is easy to get caught up in the hype cycle. Too many blockchain investors put in a ton of money because "bitcoin's going through the roof," only to see the price of bitcoin plummet the next week. Instead of "buy low, sell high," they "buy high, sell low."

In summary, this method allows you to do dollar cost averaging across both the stock market and the block market; this combination has **performed better than the stock market alone**.

At the same time, this limits our risk to the volatile blockchain markets, which can otherwise wipe out a lifetime of wealth for people who make badly-timed bets on bitcoin.

By combining traditional stock investing with a little bit of blockchain exposure, we enjoy the benefits of blockchain without betting the farm.

Source: *https://www.bitcoinmarketjournal.com/dollar-cost-average-with-bitcoin-flowchart/*

Lump Sum Investing Method

Different bitcoin investment strategies work for different people, depending on the amount of money they want to invest as well as their risk tolerance. The simplest and most widely recommended strategy is called dollar cost averaging, which involves buying the same amount of bitcoin at recurring intervals.

Another common bitcoin investment strategy is lump sum investing, which can be a preferable method of investing if you have a large amount of cash and are willing to hold onto the bitcoin for a long time. The riskiest bitcoin investment strategy is bitcoin trading, which is based on the concept of buying low and selling high. The link explains these common bitcoin investment strategies so that you can be better informed when you decide which strategy is right for you.

Source: *https://www.cryptovantage.com/news/ask-cryptovantage-whats-the-best-basic-strategy-for-bitcoin-investing/*

Crypto Hedge Fund Investing Method

If you don't want to trouble yourself with learning the basics of investing using either the dollar cost averaging method or the lump sum method, you might be better off investing your money in a cryptocurrency hedge fund. However, this option is best suited for people who can afford to pay their hefty management and performance fees.

The management fee is paid upfront; some funds require a 2%

management fee so if you're investing $100,000, $2,000 of that is going to the management fee which means only $98,000 will be invested in cryptocurrency.

Also, your hedge fund manager will get a percentage of your profits. Some managers require a 20% performance fee so if you profit $50,000 from your investment, $10,000 of that is going to be paid as an incentive fee.

The hedge fund method may not suit everyone, but if you look beyond the fees, you're at least looking at a hands-off approach to investing which could prove to be very profitable for both you and your hedge fund manager.

STRATEGIES TO SUCCEED IN BITCOIN INVESTING

Investing in Bitcoin is similar to investing in stocks. Both are high risk and high reward investments which, undoubtedly, is not for everyone.

Bitcoin is even more volatile than stocks so if you want to invest in this cryptocurrency or any other crypto for that matter, you need to know the following strategies to succeed.

Have A Solid Plan In Place

Don't invest blindly and don't invest just because everyone you know has bought Bitcoins. When investing, you need to have a good, solid plan in place where you draw your entry point and your exit point.

Your plan will need to be in accordance with the investment method you'll choose to follow. So if you choose the dollar cost averaging method, you need to have a solid plan like how much and how often you'll be buying Bitcoins.

For lump sum investing, you need to know in advance at what price you'll be buying your Bitcoins and buy at that price (don't wait for it to go any lower). For hedge fund investing, you need to consider the fees you need to pay and know the best time to invest.

Be Prepared For Volatility

This is the number one strategy you need to master. Everyone knows that Bitcoin is a highly volatile investment with prices going up and down by hundreds of dollars in mere minutes. You might think to yourself you already know it's going to be volatile because you've seen the charts and the graphs and you've practiced in a demo Bitcoin exchange account.

You can handle the risk, you tell yourself. But when you've got thousands of real dollars on the line, it's a very different scenario. Especially if you've worked hard to get those dollars! You might have worked for it for months or years, and there's a very real chance you could lose it all in just a few minutes.

The best thing you can do is to not bother with the dips at all. Just do something that will help you relax and keep your mind off Bitcoins because if you don't, you can literally go crazy. Bitcoin investing is like a roller coaster ride; you just need to hold on really, really tight until you get to the end of the ride!

Keep Calm And Don't Panic

Saying this to panicked investors is very easy, but when you're the panicked one, it's a different feeling altogether. The thought of thousands of dollars down the drain is enough to send anyone to a mental breakdown which would, of course, lead to irrational decisions.

If you don't think clearly, you might think of cutting your losses right there and then without thinking of what's going to happen in the long term. If you played your cards right, your Bitcoins would be worth so much more than when you paid for it. But you're never going to experience that if you panic and sell early.

Keep Perspective

Investing in Bitcoin is a long-term financial activity. It's different from day-today trading which involves a lot more technical analysis so a trader can make a nice profit. When investing in Bitcoin, you have zoom out of the Bitcoin price charts and look at the overall picture. Don't bother looking at the daily, weekly or monthly charts because it's going to bring you nothing but stress.

Look at how far Bitcoin rates have come. From literally a few cents when it first started to thousands of dollars now. And experts are saying this upward trend will continue for many more years to come so if you ride out the highs and lows of Bitcoin, you'll end up with a very nice investment portfolio in a few years.

Don't Spend What You Can't Lose

This is probably the most important advice you need to take note of. You already know investing in highly volatile cryptocurrencies can either make you insanely rich or bankrupt. But it doesn't have to be these two extremes.

You don't have to invest your entire fortune or your entire life savings in Bitcoin or any other cryptocurrency!

The most prudent thing you can do is to only invest what you can afford to lose. This means not spending any money that you cannot afford to lose.

Whether you choose to invest using the dollar cost averaging method, lump sum investing method, or maybe even investing in a crypto hedge fund, don't use money that needs to be used somewhere else.

If you've got money set aside for your retirement, a health fund, an emergency fund, or maybe even your kids' college money, don't even think about touching these funds. So many families have fallen apart because of wrong financial decisions and spent such important funds on risky investments.

If you've done something similar in the past and was able to get away with it, that is, you've made some profits, then don't get cocky and think you can do the same with cryptocurrency. It's a different animal, so to speak. It's the

Wild West of investments right now, and you don't want to lose your hardearned money.

Patience And Discipline Are Keys To Success

Bitcoin investing is a long-term game. You need to be patient when the Bitcoin price goes down, and your investment along with it. If you've looked at Bitcoin trends, you'll see it's been in an upward trend since its inception in 2009, so you just need to ride out the troughs until you get to the right crest where you'll be happy to sell your Bitcoins.

In the world of Bitcoin investing, there'll be many troughs and crests. You just need the discipline to hold on to your investments and not get scared when prices get too low. Likewise, don't get too excited when the price goes up. A solid plan, patience, and discipline will lead you to Bitcoin investing success.

Hindsight Is Always 20/20

Don't berate yourself if you bought at a price much higher than the current Bitcoin price. And there's no point getting angry at yourself if you sold your Bitcoins too early when the price goes up after you sold.

No one can predict the future. So the best thing for you to do is just aim to make a tidy profit and not think about the 'what ifs' because that's really not going to help you at all.

As they say, hindsight is always 20/20. To put things into perspective, if everyone can see the future, we would all have invested in Bitcoins when it was first introduced by Bitcoin founder, Satoshi Nakamoto.

ACCEPTING AND USING BITCOIN IN YOUR BUSINESS

While many online and brick-and-mortar shops and businesses have added

Bitcoin to their payment options, it's still not as widespread as the Bitcoin community would like it to be. Most business owners still prefer traditional payment methods as they simply don't know enough about Bitcoin and what they'd get out of adding it to their business.

Many don't trust Bitcoin and its volatility. They're probably thinking that with such volatile changes in the dollar-Bitcoin exchange rates, they would probably end up losing their profits. This fear is understandable, but there have been so many innovations nowadays that this really isn't a concern at all.

After all, many well-known companies like Microsoft, Overstock, Expedia, Wikipedia, Wordpress.com, Shopify, and so much more, are already accepting Bitcoin payments.

Online And Offline Businesses Can Accept Bitcoin Payments

Just because Bitcoin is a virtual currency that is electronic in nature doesn't mean that offline shops can't take advantage of receiving Bitcoin payments. For online shops, you can integrate payment processors such as Stripe,

Coinbase, Braintree, and more, into your e-commerce site's checkout page.

For offline shops, you can choose from Bitcoin terminals or Point-Of-Sale apps such as XBTerminal, Coinify or Coingate. You can also print out QR codes that your customers can scan with their mobile wallets and easily pay you in Bitcoins.

Once your Bitcoin wallet is set up, all you have to do is announce to the whole world you're ready to accept Bitcoin payments!

How To Handle The Volatility Of Bitcoin

The thought of losing your profits and essentially giving away your merchandise for free to your customers is one scary thought as you can quickly go bankrupt if all your customers paid in Bitcoin.

At one point in time it may have been true, but with Bitcoin payment processors like Coinbase and BitPay, it's now possible to receive your payments in Bitcoin and have it instantly converted to US dollars or any other supported currency. This way you avoid all the risks associated with Bitcoin and receive the full dollar amount you're supposed to receive.

To illustrate, if your customer pays you $100 worth of Bitcoin for a pair of

jeans, then you're going to receive exactly $100 in your bank account. The payment gateway you use, for example BitPay, will shield you from Bitcoin's volatility so you always get the full dollar amount.

For the more enterprising business owners who can handle Bitcoin's unpredictability, the opportunity to make even more profit from the Bitcoins they've been paid with might be irresistible.

If you belong to this category, you would probably choose to keep your Bitcoins in your digital wallets, and forego the use of a payment processor who will automatically convert your Bitcoins to dollars.

Why Your Business Should Start Accepting Bitcoin Payments

Bitcoin was created by Satoshi Nakamoto in response to the 2008 financial market crash which almost crippled the entire global economy. He created it to solve or overcome the problems we have with having a centralized banking system that benefited banks more than they did consumers.

Just think about the bank fees you have to pay everytime someone pays you for your product or service. Deposit fees, withdrawal fees, transaction fees, credit card fees, and all sorts of fees are deducted from your hardearned money.

Bitcoin's purpose was to avoid all that, and this peer-to-peer electronic cash system was Satoshi Nakamoto's solution to the problem. The system was created essentially so that everyone gets what is due them without the unnecessary intervention of banks and government.

The Benefits Of Bitcoin Payments For Your Business

There are plenty of benefits for your business if you choose to start accepting Bitcoin payments. Here are some of them:

No Risk Of Chargebacks

Paypal, credit and debit card payments leave your business vulnerable to chargebacks. Most, if not all, businesses (both online and offline merchants) have probably experienced this problem at one point or another. Dealing with a chargeback is a headache-inducing and timeconsuming process.

Your customers can claim to not recognize the charge on their card statements, or their card was stolen and somebody else used it to buy from

you, or they're upset that your merchandise was not as described or it was defective.

Some people simply like to do chargebacks because they want to get an item for free, especially if it's a high-value item. Of course, this is a very unethical thing to do, but you can't predict your customers' behaviors.

With Bitcoin payments, there is zero risk of chargebacks because all payments, once it has been confirmed, are final. There is no way for anyone, not even the savviest and smartest programmers in the world, can reverse or undo a Bitcoin transaction.

Bitcoin payments offer merchant protection that is unparalleled by any other payment option available today. No bank and no government can give you the level of merchant protection that Bitcoin does.

No Fraud And Double Payments

The Bitcoin network is an extremely secure payment system. Unlike banks, Bitcoin is incorruptible. Before Bitcoin came along, double payments and fraud were a very real problem with digital cash but luckily, thanks to the efforts of Satoshi Nakamoto, the problem of double spending was finally solved.

Bitcoin is a decentralized, peer-to-peer payment system. Everyone on the network sees all the Bitcoin transactions that have ever taken place. This transparency makes it difficult for fraudsters to fake records so they can spend the same amount of Bitcoins twice or double spend it.

This massive ledger, also known as the blockchain, keeps a record of all transactions. A transaction is only added to a block once it has been confirmed or verified by miners that the transaction is valid.

Near Instant Payments

Bitcoin payments are fast, irrevocable and final. There's no way for anyone to undo any Bitcoin transaction. As long you indicate the correct Bitcoin address for your customers to pay into, you're good to go, and your Bitcoins will arrive in your wallet usually within 10-45 minutes.

Using the correct Bitcoin address is obviously a very important point to consider because if by any chance, you present the wrong Bitcoin address, then there's no way for you to recover those Bitcoins. Unless of course, you know who owns that Bitcoin address, then you can simply ask them to send those Bitcoins to your correct address.

Another upside to using payment gateways like Coinbase and BitPay is that you can receive your cash in your bank accounts within 2-3 days. These services usually send payments every business day (not everytime a transaction occurs).

Alternatively, if you want to keep your Bitcoins, that is, you don't want to convert them to dollars, then that's perfectly fine. You can select this option in your payment gateway settings. Either way, you're going to get your Bitcoins or your dollars very conveniently and in less time than if the customer paid with Paypal or a credit card.

Negligible Transaction Fees

With Bitcoin payments, you get to keep more of what your customer pays you. You effectively cut out the middleman (your bank) with their expensive fees. You will still need to pay a very small Bitcoin transaction fee which goes to the miners who verify all Bitcoin transactions and add it to the ledger or blockchain.

This transaction fee is almost negligible and is a mere equivalent to cents, unlike the fees your bank or credit card company requires you to pay!

For credit card payments, merchants are usually charged an interchange fee (paid to the bank or card issuer) and an assessment fee (paid to the credit card company such as Visa or Mastercard). On average, these fees will end up costing the merchant around 3% to 4% per transaction.

In comparison, for Bitcoin transactions, the fees are typically around 10,000

Satoshis or 0.0001 Bitcoin. You're free to set your own fees, but the higher the transaction fee you set per transaction, the faster Bitcoin miners will confirm your transaction.

For a $1,000 credit card payment, the fees that merchants have to pay would be around $30 to $40. For a similar purchase amount paid for in Bitcoin, the transaction fee would roughly be around $1 if the current Bitcoin price is say, for example, $10,000 per Bitcoin ($10,000 x 0.0001 = $1).

You can already see just by this example that Bitcoin transactions will save you a lot of money just in transaction fees. Imagine how much you will get to save if you're able to sell your $1,000 product just 10 times a day or 100 times a day!

Increased Sales and More Profit for You

Bitcoin doesn't discriminate where anyone comes from. Even if your customer lives in a country known for credit card fraud, in Bitcoin's eyes everyone is equal. If you've ever tried to accept payments from customers in these countries, you know just how difficult and cumbersome the entire process is.

PayPal, Stripe, and other popular payment gateways don't accept or support many countries with high prevalence of fraud. But with Bitcoin, you can easily accept payments from anyone who lives anywhere in the world. All they need to pay you is just your Bitcoin address!

They don't need to send their photos and national ID cards, so your customers' privacy is well protected. And as you already know, all Bitcoin transactions are final, so there's no way for any of your customers to do a chargeback like they easily can with a credit card.

Bitcoin makes the world a smaller and better place. It erases borders, government red tape, and bureaucracy. It allows merchants and business owners like you to receive payments from customers who are unfortunate enough to live in countries with a high fraud rate.

Bitcoin protects you and your business. At the same time, it allows you to provide your service and your products to everyone in the whole world.

Happier Customers

Adding Bitcoin to your list of supported payments will give your customers an extra choice to hand over their money to you. Even if they don't have Bitcoins yet, they might eventually get into the game sooner or later.

And when they do, they'll remember you and recommend you to their friends. Even existing customers will be happy to know you've added Bitcoin payments.

If you're one of the few businesses in your community that accepts Bitcoin payments, then you're probably going to become popular because you'll be viewed as an innovative and forward-thinking business.

Many people have heard about Bitcoin on the news, and many would have developed a passing interest or have begun to become curious about Bitcoins and cryptocurrency in general. You can educate your customers and let them know what Bitcoin is and how it will help them in their financial transactions.

Think about it, would you rather be one of the first businesses to offer

Bitcoin payments and steal your competitor's customers in the process? Or would you rather have your customers go to your competition simply because they offer Bitcoin payments, and you don't?

Get Support from The Bitcoin Community

The Bitcoin community is growing fast, and with skyrocketing Bitcoin prices, they are looking for places where they can spend their Bitcoins. Several big companies have added Bitcoin to their payment options, but a great majority of businesses have yet to follow suit. So, when the Bitcoin community discovers a new business that supports Bitcoin, they share the news with everyone. That's free advertisement for your business, and you can expect them to drop by your website or physical store anytime soon.

To get sufficient exposure to the Bitcoin community, you can spread the news on social media, in Bitcoin forums, pages, groups, etc. If you have a physical store, you should also put a large signboard outside that will announce to anyone passing by that you're accepting Bitcoin payments.

Growing your business doesn't have to be difficult. Accepting Bitcoin payments will not only make your business popular among the Bitcoin community, but it will also lead to more sales and more profits for you.

How to Protect Yourself Against Fraud and Theft

Bitcoin and cryptocurrencies are hot commodities right now. Everyone wants a piece of the action, though with soaring prices, many can't afford to buy and invest out of their own pockets.

So, they do the next best thing they can think of – scam and steal these precious digital coins from other people. In this guide, we'll show you some of the most common scams these con artists are running as well as how you can protect yourself against them.

Bitcoin and Cryptocurrencies are Not Scams

Before we go into the main scams you should be aware of, we'd like to point out that these scams are all from outside forces, and not cryptocurrencies themselves. You might hear some people say that cryptocurrencies are nothing but a huge scam but it's 100% false, and we'll explain why.

The technology behind cryptocurrencies is called the blockchain. It is an incorruptible digital ledger that records all transactions in the network. No central body controls it. It is transparent, and anyone can track any transaction that has ever happened in the past.

No one can alter any transaction recorded on the blockchain because doing so would mean you'd have to alter the rest of the transactions or blocks that came after that particular transaction; this is virtually an impossible task to do.

The blockchain is so secure that many banks and startup companies are now experimenting, and starting to implement blockchain technology

because they've seen just how well it works on Bitcoin and cryptocurrencies.

Now that you know you can trust the technology behind cryptocurrencies, let's discuss the most common scams that many people fall prey to.

Scam #1 – Fake Bitcoin Exchanges

There are plenty of reputable Bitcoin exchanges today. The biggest and most popular platforms that have been around a few years are Coinbase, Kraken, CEX.io, Changelly, Bitstamp, Poloniex, and Bitfinex. With that being said, we cannot vouch for any company even if they're well known in the industry.

You will have to do your due diligence by researching the company's history, user reviews, and determine for yourself whether you want to spend your hard-earned fiat money with them.

Too Good to Be True Exchange Rates

Due to the highly volatile nature of cryptocurrencies (prices can go up and down by a huge spread in just a few hours!), many unsavory characters on the Internet are capitalizing on this volatility. They prey on unsuspecting beginners who can't spot the difference between a legitimate exchange and a fake one.

These fake Bitcoin exchanges can easily put up nice-looking websites and impress people with their seemingly sophisticated look. They hook people in with their promises of lower-than-market-rate prices and guaranteed returns. Simply put, they play on people's greed.

Imagine how ecstatic you'd feel if you found out about a website that offers Bitcoins at 10% or 20% lower rates than the going rates on Coinbase or Kraken. If these large platforms are offering $15,000 for 1 Bitcoin, and this other site is offering it at $12,000, wouldn't you jump at the chance?

You'd save so much ($3,000 per Bitcoin!), and you can use your savings to buy even more Bitcoins. See, that's them playing on greed! They know that people want to buy more Bitcoins for less dollars. And who can blame those

poor victims? If we didn't know any better, we might fall for the same scam too.

Receive Instant PayPal Payment for Your Bitcoins

Another method these fake Bitcoin exchanges use to steal your Bitcoins is they'll offer to buy your coins at higher-than-market-rates, and then send the equivalent dollar amount to your PayPal address.

To the unsuspecting Bitcoin owner, he thinks he's getting the better end of the deal because he's going to get more money for his Bitcoins, and he'll get the cash instantly in his PayPal account.

So, he enters the amount of Bitcoins he wants to sell, confirms he's happy with the equivalent dollar amount, types in his PayPal address so they can send the money to him, then he waits. And waits. And waits some more.

He'll contact the website but, of course, they're not going to reply to him now because they have his Bitcoins (remember, all Bitcoin transactions are final and irreversible once validated).

At this point, he'll realize he's just been scammed. He can report the site and write bad reviews, but who's he kidding? These savvy scammers will just set up shop under a new domain name and wait for their next victim.

The key takeaway here is to stay away from 'exchanges' with too-good-tobe-true rates. As the saying goes, if it's too good to be true, it probably is.

Scam #2 – Phishing Scams

There are so many kinds of phishing scams that run rampant today. Ever received an email from your 'bank' asking you verify or update your account details to make sure your details remain up to date? And that you must click on the email link to update your details?

Many people are aware these types of emails are nothing more than a scam. Modern email services send these junk emails to the junk folder anyway, so you don't see them all that much nowadays.

But with Bitcoin and cryptocurrency being so new and so hot in the news right now, scammers are scrambling to find a way to steal your Bitcoins by getting access to your digital wallets!

Email Phishing Scams

Scammers will send you an email designed to make it look like it came from your online wallet service (therefore we don't suggest storing large sums of virtual currency in your exchange wallets).

In the email, they'll ask you to click on a link which will lead you to a fake website. It will look exactly like your exchange or wallet website. Of course, it's not the same because the domain name will be different.

For example, if you're using Coinbase, they'll use a similar misspelled domain such as:

Cooinbase

Coiinbase

Coinbasse

Coinsbase

Coinbase-Client-Update.com

or something similar…

It will also most probably not have a security feature called SSL installed, which means the domain will start with HTTP and not HTTPS (modern browsers like Chrome and Firefox should warn you if it's a secure site or not).

If you fall for this phishing scam, and you log in to the fake wallet site, then the scammers now have your login details to your real wallet! They can easily lock you out of your account, and they'll then have the freedom to transfer every single Bitcoin you own to their own wallets.

Malware Scams

In this type of scam, scammers will ask you to click on a link either via email, banner ad, forum ad, or anywhere they can post a link which will then download a type of malware to your computer.

Often, these malwares are keyloggers which will record everything you type on your computer and send the information to the scammers. So, if you log in to your online wallet, like Coinbase for example, they will be able to see your username and your password, and they can then log in to your account and easily steal your coins from you!

The key takeaway for protecting yourself from these types of scams is to never click on links from untrustworthy sources.

If you don't recognize the sender, or the website domain name is misspelled, it should raise a red flag, and you should report the email and/or leave the phishing site right away.

Furthermore, consider using offline storing methods such as paper wallets or hardware wallets so even if scammers get access to your online wallet, they'll have nothing to steal there.

Scam #3 – Cloud Mining Scams

Cloud mining is a popular way of becoming a Bitcoin miner. You no longer need to invest in your own supercomputer and join a mining group to solve complex cryptographic hash problems. You don't even need to worry about expensive electricity bills.

You simply need to sign up to a cloud mining service (also known as a mining farm), rent mining equipment, and receive payments proportionate to your subscription.

While some cloud mining companies are legitimate, there are many fly-bynight websites which promise unrealistic returns for measly sums, whose sole purpose is to steal your money.

Some common red flags to watch out for when looking to join a cloud mining service is the absence of an About page, Terms of Use/Service page, physical address, and/or contact number.

They might also not have a secure domain (no HTTPS before their domain name). These details are all very important in figuring out which site is a scam, and which is not. You can search Google for reviews and go through

their website to get a feel if they're legitimate or not. Often, these sites would be anonymous with no names or faces behind them.

Some may appear legitimate at first but take a deeper look at what your

investment's going to get you. You may pay eventually sign up for a contract which is going to cost you a few thousand dollars a year but what are you going to get in return? You'll have to do the math yourself and calculate if you're going to end up in the green.

The key takeaway here is before you spend any of your hard-earned fiat money, you should at least make sure you're dealing with a legitimate company and not some anonymous scammer who'll leave you in tears.

Do plenty of research, read reviews, and browse the crypto-mining communities for information on the best and most trustworthy cloud mining companies.

Scam #4 – Ponzi Scams

Ponzi scams are probably easier to spot than the other scams we've covered so far in this guide. This is because Ponzi scams are well known for guaranteeing outlandish returns on investments with little to no risk to the investors. People fall for these sorts of scams all the time because people want guaranteed returns on their investments.

With Bitcoin and cryptocurrency, any company that guarantees exponential returns on any investment should be viewed as a potential scammer. The cryptocurrency market is highly volatile, and one minute the price could be at an all-time high and the next, it's down by a few hundred or a few thousand dollars.

Because of this volatility, you should never believe anyone who tells you you're guaranteed a 10% return on your investment every single day, or whatever the scammer's terms may be.

Since Ponzi schemes rely on new members, a.k.a. victims, to pay off their early investors, they usually offer incentives for members to recruit new people to join their network.

It's very common for scams like this to offer some form of affiliate rewards.

You refer someone to invest in the 'company,' and you get compensated for your efforts.

Some Ponzi schemes guarantee daily profits *forever*. If this seems impossible, it most certainly is. No one even knows if Bitcoins will be around that long and guaranteeing daily returns is just crazy. Right off the bat, an intelligent investor will see that offers like these are nothing more than scams designed to rip you off your money or your Bitcoins.

In fact, many of these scam sites prefer Bitcoin payments because they know Bitcoin transactions can't be reversed or canceled once sent! Either way, whether they require fiat or cryptocurrency, know who you're sending your money to first.

The key takeaway here is if you know the company's offers are too good to be true, then you should run away in the opposite direction. Sometimes, there's just no point in even looking up reviews on the Internet when it comes to scams like these because most 'reviewers' are those who got in the game early and thus have already received some return on their investment.

And usually, when these users leave reviews, they'll include their affiliate link so you know right away they have a vested interest for leaving glowing reviews for a company they may, or may not know, is a scam.

THE FUTURE OF CRYPTOCURRENCY

Before we talk about the future of cryptocurrency, it's important to remind ourselves of the past and what cryptocurrency was like in the beginning. Back in 2008, when Bitcoin founder, Satoshi Nakamoto, first released his whitepaper on Bitcoin, many people said it was just a fad and a scam designed to trick people into giving up their 'real' money.

There were many naysayers and financial experts who said Bitcoin will never be adopted by the masses and will fizzle and die out in a year or so.

Fortunately, the cryptocurrency community rallied and worked together to make Bitcoin a success. They saw potential in the blockchain technology and what it could mean for the finance sector. They saw the need for cryptocurrency because the current financial setup via banks and governments had too many problems and was causing national economies to collapse.

They saw that keeping inflation at bay was difficult with traditional currencies and the poorest people often have no easy access to banks. Receiving or sending payments was oftentimes a headache with transaction fees eating up a significant amount of money.

Banks charge exorbitant fees just so their customers can get access to their very own money, and the government takes very little action, if at all, to help the people.

Bitcoin supporters say the modern financial system is a mess where banks and governments collude or work together, not to help their citizens' financial needs, but to take as much money as they can from them in terms of fees collected.

Bitcoin changed all that. With Bitcoin, you're cutting out the middleman. There are no more banks to deal with and no government to spy on your bank accounts. With Bitcoin, you are your own bank. You're the bank teller sending and receiving payments, and you're the banker in charge of keeping your money safe.

Bitcoin has been a leader on so many fronts. As the first successful cryptocurrency, it has paved the way for other cryptocurrencies to succeed and the global community has slowly taken notice these past few years. Read on to find out what other possibilities Bitcoin and cryptocurrencies bring for the future!

UNDERDEVELOPED COUNTRIES

In most developed countries, getting a credit card or a business loan is relatively easy. However, in developing countries, you'd have to literally jump through hoops and government red tape before you can get one. But with Bitcoin and cryptocurrency, all you need is just your digital wallet, and you can start receiving cryptocurrency from anyone, anywhere in the world.

You don't even need your own Internet connection at home; you can simply go somewhere with good Internet access and create a quick wallet online or on your mobile phone. Of course, storing your crypto online is not a good idea so you should investigate storing these in cold storage, such as a hardware wallet or paper wallet.

But online wallets are great for small transactions so if you need to pay a utility bill or your credit card bill, simply scan the utility company's Bitcoin wallet's QR code and send your crypto payment. No need to spend the whole day standing in long lines!

Today, there are already many businesses which have started to accept Bitcoin payments (though they are still in the minority). These forward-thinking business owners see the benefit of accepting Bitcoins and are profiting nicely from this smart business decision!

You can buy virtually anything with Bitcoins. You can buy plane tickets, you can rent cars, you can pay for your college tuition, you can buy groceries, you can buy stuff on Amazon by purchasing Amazon gift cards on third-party sites, and so much more!

In the future, we can expect so many more businesses to jump onto the Bitcoin payment wagon, and it would be a win-win situation for both business owners and customers.

Businesses will get their payment fast and into their bank accounts the very next day (using a payment gateway like BitPay which offers instant Bitcoins to fiat currency conversion), and customers will get to buy items in a very convenient manner.

Bitcoin in Developing Economies

It's not surprising that Bitcoin has seen massive adoption in recent years. In fact, in Zimbabwe, people are using Bitcoins to make financial transactions. With the demise of the Zimbabwean dollar, the country had to resort to using US dollars as their main currency.

However, this is not a very feasible solution because their government can't print US dollars themselves. Venezuelans are also experiencing the same problem. The Venezuelan bolivar has become so hyper-inflated it's almost unusable. People have resorted to using Bitcoins to pay for basic goods, medicines, groceries, and so much more.

For the Zimbabweans and Venezuelans, as well as the Vietnamese, Colombians, and citizens of countries with super inflated currencies, Bitcoin

is a beacon of light because it's not subject to the whims and manipulations of their local banks or their governments.

Their present economic situation is a perfect example of the downside of

having a central authority to manage a country's currency, while at the same time, it highlights all the benefits of using Bitcoin, a decentralized and 100% transparent financial network.

With Bitcoin getting massive support from people in developing countries, governments may soon be stepping in to regulate the use of Bitcoin and other cryptocurrencies. While we can't predict the future, for now, Bitcoin provides a wonderful inflation-less alternative to traditional currency.

And with skyrocketing Bitcoin and cryptocurrency prices, this gives many people a lot of purchasing power which their national currencies can't provide.

Fast and Cheap International Payments

One of the main benefits of Bitcoin payments is the speed by which the recipient can get their Bitcoins. This is perfect for people who hire freelancers or employees overseas.

The employees don't need to sign up for a bank account and incur fees left and right just because they're receiving money from yourself, an international client.

Of course, we must not fail to mention the fees that you yourself will be paying to your bank everytime you remit or transfer monies to your overseas workers.

In addition to the fees both you and your recipient pay, you'd also have to factor in the exchange rate. Most banks and money transfer services will usually tell you up front that "this" is the current exchange rate but when you compare it to actual rates, the bank rate would be much lower.

Even for PayPal payments, you'll notice a difference in the exchange rate they use. You probably won't notice the exchange rate when you're transferring relatively small amounts, but when you're transacting in thousands of dollars, the fees can very quickly add up to a significant amount.

With Bitcoin, you can say goodbye to all these exorbitant fees.

For every Bitcoin transaction, you do need to pay a small fee for the miners, but it's literally nothing compared to what your banks are charging you!

Whether you're sending 1,000 Bitcoins or 0.01 Bitcoins, the mining fee can be the same since the fee is computed in terms of bytes, not the amount of Bitcoins.

The size (in bytes) of your transaction will depend on the number of inputs and outputs per transaction. Without going into the technical details, what's important to take note here is the mining fees are very, very small compared to your bank's fees. Therefore, Bitcoin and cryptocurrency are going to change the future. More people will transact with each other directly to avoid paying those very expensive bank fees!

With more and more people sending cryptocurrency to each other directly, there may be no more need for third-party money transfer services or even

banks. Though this may take many years to happen, it's still a possibility once everyone gets educated on the benefits of using cryptocurrency to send and receive payments from anyone in the world in just a few minutes.

CORRUPTION AND CRIME

Many people are worried that the Bitcoin network is being used by money launderers, criminals, and corrupt officials because they think it's an anonymous network. Yes, all verified transactions are recorded on the blockchain and no, there are no names listed there.

You can see only alphanumeric codes, lots of it in fact. If you download the free and open source Bitcoin Core client, you'll also need to download the entire blockchain which is already more than 100GB+. Millions of Bitcoin transactions since 2009 are stored on the blockchain. You'll even see the first ever transaction by its founder, Satoshi Nakamoto.

We're mentioning this to point to the fact that Bitcoin is not anonymous. Instead, it's pseudonymous, meaning users can hide behind pseudonyms, but on close inspection, digital forensics experts can trace who owns Bitcoin wallets.

This is, of course, a time-consuming endeavor but when you're after criminals who've laundered millions or billions of dollars' worth of Bitcoins then catching them becomes a top priority. In fact, experts say that criminals are better off stashing their stolen loot in offshore bank accounts with their super strict bank privacy laws.

But Bitcoin is easier to move around so people think they can easily hide their illicit transactions in the alphanumeric maze known as the blockchain. In short, several criminals have been put behind bars thanks to Bitcoin and the blockchain.

In the future, if and when cryptocurrency gains massive support and adoption from the masses worldwide, it will be easier for authorities to trace and catch criminals hoping to use cryptocurrencies as a means to hide and move their stolen money around.

BLOCKCHAIN TECHNOLOGY IS BECOMING MAINSTREAM

Many governments, banks, and private organizations are looking into adopting the blockchain technology into their products and services. The blockchain is the underlying technology behind Bitcoin and other cryptocurrencies.

The technology is already starting to receive recognition and adoption from many sectors in the world. While this may take several years, it's at least a positive nod in favor of the blockchain revolution.

Two of the most popular blockchain technologies today are Ethereum and Hyperledger. You may have heard of Ethereum as the second most

popular cryptocurrency, after Bitcoin. But it's more than just a virtual currency platform.

Ethereum is a platform that allows anyone to create smart contracts which help people trade or exchange anything of value, such as money, property, stocks, etc. The contract is publicly transparent and is recorded on the blockchain which means other people are witness to the agreement.

The best thing about smart contracts is you are basically automating contracts without paying for the services of a middleman such as a bank, stockbroker, or lawyer.

Hyperledger, on the other hand, is an open source, cross-industry collaborative project with contributors from many major companies such as Deutsche Bank, IBM, Airbus and SAP.

According to their website, the collaboration aims to develop a "new generation of transactional applications that establish trust, accountability and transparency." These applications have the potential to streamline business processes and reduce the cost and complexity of various systems in the real world.

These are just a few examples of how blockchain technology is going to change the world in the future. Blockchain may be less than a decade old, but it has already changed the lives of so many people for the better.

THE CRYPTOCURRENCY REVOLUTION

In this guide, you've learned so many benefits of using Bitcoin, cryptocurrency and blockchain technology. Investing in cryptocurrency may be in your best interest though it's always best to do in-depth research on which cryptocurrency to invest in.

Bitcoin may be too expensive for now but remember that you don't have to buy a whole Bitcoin. Alternatively, there are other emerging cryptocurrencies with good track records you may consider investing in.

With cryptocurrency looking set to get integrated with mainstream financial markets, investing in cryptocurrency is not a scary thought anymore. In fact, it just might be the best financial decision you'll ever make for yourself and your family's future.

CONCLUSION

There have been few discoveries and inventions over the course of history that have made long-lasting impacts on the direction and pace of human progress. Blockchain technology promises to be one such invention.

The promise that is holds for redefining air travel, ocean freight, and global logistics and what it can do to transform healthcare by providing safe and secure medical records, as well as the opportunities in the fields of microfinance,

finance, credit investments, and prediction markets, suggests that the world is slowly waking up to what blockchain technology can do.

The capabilities of this emerging technology are still being determined, and there is still a lot of work that still needs to be done. Millions of dollars in investments are being poured into this area of research and development, and every day we see new blockchain-based ideas, startups, and initiatives being launched, with each one hoping to be the one that will catch fire and transform the way things are done.

Now is the time for a change, and new blockchain technology is powering the drive to change. However, as we move forward, we need to take cautious steps to ensure that we use the technology in the right way and deliver as much benefit to as many people as possible.

If you are looking considering utilizing blockchain technology for your business, the only way that you will truly master it is if you dedicate yourself to becoming a lifelong learner in the space.

In this guide, you will learn all about Bitcoin (BTC) and cryptocurrency, how they work, why they exist and what kind of technology is behind Bitcoin. It wasn't too long ago when people started hearing the words 'Bitcoin' and 'cryptocurrencies.'

Few people outside of the crypto communities knew what they were, and many thought it was just another fad that was bound to fail in a few years or so. The value of one Bitcoin was just a few cents then so obviously it wasn't worth a lot. For this reason, it was ignored by the masses. There were far more profitable investments one could make, after all.

Those who invested sums of money on the new digital currency either believed in the system proposed by its founder, Satoshi Nakamoto, or they simply wanted to see how it works.

Either way, those who believed were rewarded greatly, and continue to be rewarded, as a single Bitcoin now costs thousands of dollars.

It only took Bitcoin five years to breach the $1,000 mark in late 2013, and just a few years later, Bitcoin prices are at an all-time high – way past the $10,000 mark for a single Bitcoin!

With skyrocketing prices and extremely fast growth, more and more people are curious about Bitcoins and cryptocurrencies.

TOP 10 CRYPTOCURRENCIES BY MARKET CAPITALIZATION

Valid as of Feb 2021

https://coinmarketcap.com/

Rank	Name	Symbol	Market Cap	Price	Circulating Supply	Volume (24h)	% 1h	% 24h	% 7d
1	Bitcoin	BTC	$1,000,211,537,586	$53,679.61	18,632,987 BTC	$55,901,974,625	1.79%	3.13%	15.53%
2	Ethereum	ETH	$221,977,314,017	$1,934.68	114,735,960 ETH	$25,838,576,539	0.60%	0.89%	10.13%
3	Binance Coin	BNB	$47,964,884,412	$310.39	154,532,785 BNB *	$15,537,198,290	4.63%	60.66%	140.57%
4	Tether	USDT	$33,538,609,548	$1.00	33,531,193,546 USDT *	$107,650,248,145	0.00%	0.02%	-0.04%
5	Polkadot	DOT	$32,822,619,396	$33.85	969,607,870 DOT *	$3,119,390,722	1.33%	7.78%	29.35%
6	Cardano	ADA	$28,603,951,356	$0.9194	31,112,484,646 ADA	$4,730,944,545	-0.55%	-1.51%	7.11%
7	XRP	XRP	$25,106,670,911	$0.9530	45,404,028,640 XRP *	$6,456,859,759	-1.45%	2.97%	-1.80%
8	Litecoin	LTC	$15,360,081,444	$230.91	66,521,067 LTC	$6,756,759,757	0.83%	0.61%	27.75%
9	Chainlink	LINK	$13,944,787,176	$34.26	407,009,556 LINK *	$2,166,621,851	1.04%	4.80%	24.50%
10	Bitcoin Cash	BCH	$13,512,472,093	$724.16	18,659,475 BCH	$4,655,649,178	0.04%	2.21%	37.22%

TOP 10 SPOT MARKET EXCHANGES

Valid as of Feb 2021

https://coinmarketcap.com/rankings/exchanges/

#	Name	Exchange Score	Volume(24h)	Avg. Liquidity	Visits - Similarweb	# Markets	# Coins	Fiat Supported	Volume Graph (7d)
1	Binance	8.9	$36,060,400,628 + 24.48%	616	12,970,426	1051	330	AED, ARS, AUD and +43 more	
2	Coinbase Pro	8.6	$3,519,045,656 + 0.83%	489	11,671,937	129	46	USD, EUR, GBP	
3	Kraken	8.4	$1,659,718,191 + 1.02%	533	2,745,278	271	60	USD, EUR, GBP and +4 more	
4	Huobi Global	8.3	$7,319,724,611 + 2.58%	424	664,543	914	312	--	
5	Bitfinex	8.2	$1,183,249,282 + 11.71%	490	592,746	270	143	USD, EUR, GBP and +1 more	
6	KuCoin	8.4	$736,471,577 + 26.73%	396	452,290	586	273	TOKEN	
7	Bithumb	8.0	$3,545,612,278 + 16.28%	251	1,018,101	161	152	KRW	
8	Bitstamp	7.9	$800,000,166 + 5.67%	288	525,305	42	13	USD, EUR, GBP	
9	Binance.US	8.7	$897,478,027 + 42.64%	276	744,489	108	54	USD	
10	Bittrex	7.6	$287,567,517 + 1.06%	327	903,850	635	324	USD	

TOP 30 CRYPTOCURRENCY NAMES, ACRONYMS AND SYMBOLS

Bitcoin BTC

Ethereum ETH

Binance Coin BNB

Tether USDT

Polkadot DOT

Cardano ADA

XRP XRP

Litecoin LTC

Chainlink LINK

Bitcoin Cash BCH

Stellar XLM

USD Coin USDC

Dogecoin DOGE

Wrapped Bitcoin WBTC

Uniswap UNI

Aave AAVE

EOS EOS

Cosmos ATOM

Monero XMR

Bitcoin SV BSV

TRON TRX

NEM XEM

IOTA MIOTA

Huobi Token HT

Tezos XTZ

THETA THETA

VeChain VET

Neo NEO

Dash DASH

Crypto.com Coin CRO

www.ingramcontent.com/pod-product-compliance
Lightning Source LLC
Chambersburg PA
CBHW071139050326
40690CB00008B/1507